*W*ILD FLOWERS
IN CROSS STITCH
Jane Iles

BY THE SAME AUTHOR:
The Needlework Garden

WILD FLOWERS
IN CROSS STITCH
Jane Iles

BLITZ

For Dan and Sarah Jane

First published in 1990 by Random Century Group,
20 Vauxhall Bridge Road, London SW1V 2SA

Published in 1993 by Blitz Editions an imprint of Bookmart Limited
Registered Number 2372865
Trading as Bookmart Limited, Desford Road,
Enderby, Leicester LE9 5AD

Design by Clare Clements

Location photographs by Julie Fisher
Styling by Jacky Boase

Still-life photographs by Rosemary Weller
Propping by Doris Partridge

Charts by Colin Salmon
Additional artworks by Anthony Duke
Illustrations by Sally Holmes

Typeset by DP Photosetting, Aylesbury, Bucks
Printed and bound by
New Interlitho S.p.a., Milan, Italy

British Library Cataloguing in Publication Data
Iles, Jane
Wild Flowers in cross - stitch
1. Embroidery. Cross - stitch
I. Title
746.44

ISBN 1 85605 084 X

CONTENTS

INTRODUCTION

Wild flowers have always attracted me with their pure colours and simple shapes. To see a wild flower growing and hopefully flourishing in its natural habitat is a stirring sight which has provided the inspiration behind the designs in this book.

To capture the beautiful simplicity of wild flowers and plants, Cross Stitch has been chosen as the means of interpreting their colour and form, so ensuring that the design emphasises the flowers rather than losing them in complicated techniques and textures.

Cross Stitch is one of the oldest types of embroidery (decorative stitchery) and examples of it, both old and new, can be seen all over the world. It has always been particularly popular with peasant communities where it has been used in vivid colours to brighten and enhance everyday clothes as well as household and ceremonial items.

In this book Cross Stitch has been chosen for its simplicity of construction, with emphasis being laid upon the colour of thread and more importantly upon the design itself. The only other embroidery stitch that has been used is Back Stitch when a fine single line is required, such as for the roots of a plant.

To work the designs most effectively evenweave fabric or canvas has been used, as this ensures that the design is transferred from the chart to the fabric accurately and without distortion of the shapes. The fabrics used are specifically named to help you to purchase the correct one for each project. However, always remember that with a little careful experimentation and adjustment to the instructions you can easily and effectively adapt any of the designs in this book. Change to a different fabric or thread and you will be able to use each design for a variety of projects.

Jane Lees.

CONVOLVULUS

*This fast-growing plant, commonly known
as bindweed, can be found thriving along railway
banks, road sides, farmland and other
cultivated land. Its attractive trumpet-like flowers
provide a delightful design for the
entwined pattern on the cushion and hand towel.*

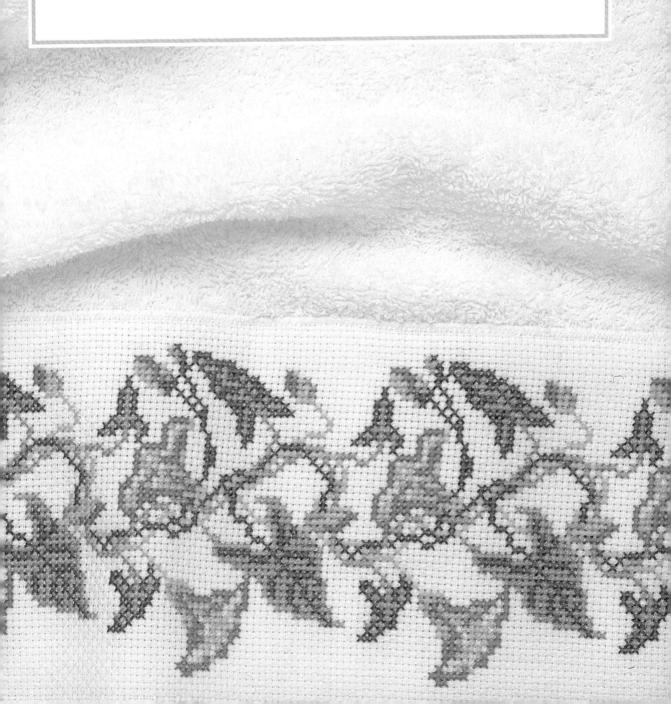

CONVOLVULUS HAND TOWEL

The all-over repeat pattern of the canvaswork cushion on page 22 has been simply adapted so that it can be used to give a linear pattern of a single group of entwined stems twisting and curling around each other along the border of this pretty hand towel.

MATERIALS

White hand towel, 56cm (22in) wide
White Fine Aida fabric (Zweigart 14 count E3706), 20 × 70cm (8 × 28in)
DMC stranded embroidery thread:
    1 skein each Green 472, 704, 905;
    Pink 776, 819, 961
White sewing thread
Small rotating frame, or wooden
    embroidery hoop, 15cm (6in) in
    diameter

TO MAKE THE TOWEL BORDER

If you look at the chart on page 25 for the convolvulus cushion and compare it with the chart on page 18 for the towel border you will see that they are very similar. The border design has been adapted to make an all-over pattern for the cushion. For the border simply repeat the chart on page 18 over and over again.

1 If you are using a rotating frame mount the short ends of the Fine Aida fabric on the rotating sides of the frame and roll the excess fabric around one of these sides. If you are using a hoop place one end of the strip within the hoop (you will find that you will have to reposition this several times as you work the border).

2 Find the centre of the width of the fabric and mark it temporarily with a dressmaker's pin, this will help you position your Cross Stitch border design centrally along the strip of fabric.

3 Use *two* strands of thread while you work the towel. Remember to work your Cross Stitches so that all the upper stitches face the same way to produce an even effect.

Whether it's bindweed, convolvulus or morning glory, the entwined stems of these plants are a perfect design source.

961

776

819

905

704

472

Repeat this chart over and over again along the fabric strip to make the towel border.

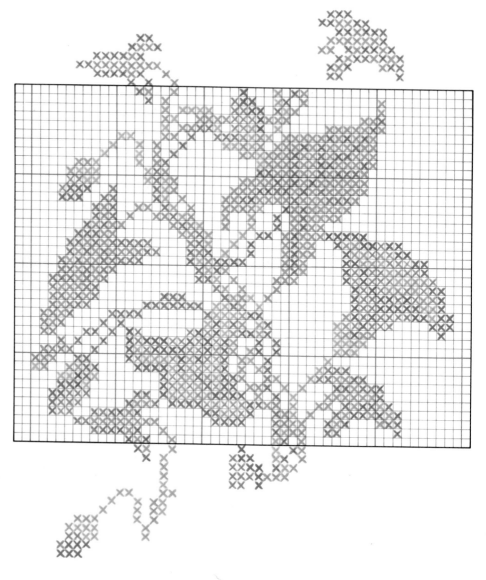

4 Work along the length of the strip, repeating the design nearly eight complete times. When nearing the end of the strip, measure the exact width of your hand towel and work the border to fit.

5 Remove the fabric from the frame or hoop and press it carefully on the wrong side, using a steam iron. This will encourage the stitchery to stand out on the right side.

6 With the Cross Stitch border centrally positioned, cut away the surplus fabric at either side to give a strip which is 11cm (4½in) wide. Similarly trim the surplus fabric at the ends of the border, leaving 1cm (⅜in) at each end for a small turning.

7 Pin and baste the Cross Stitch border across one end of the towel, tucking in the turned allowance at both ends. With white sewing thread, machine Satin Stitch along the raw edges of the border, covering them completely with the width of the Satin Stitching and attaching the strip to the towel securely.

8 Finally, Slip Stitch the turned allowances to the towel sides to complete your convolvulus hand towel.

MORNING GLORY
SCENTED SACHET

By simply changing the colour of the flowers this design can be changed from the bindweed plant to the morning glory or ipomoea, which will grow successfully in sheltered gardens where it can enjoy the early morning sunshine. In its native Mediterranean habitat it will grow freely like the bindweed and quickly establish itself.

This charming scented sachet shows how effective the change of colour can be. The cushion and hand towel could also be worked using shades of mauve instead of pink for the flowers.

MATERIALS
White Fine Aida fabric (Zweigart
   E3706), 25cm (10in) square
Printed cotton fabric suitable for back
   of sachet, 16cm (6¼in) square
2 pieces of white cotton lining fabric,
   each 16cm (6¼in) square
DMC stranded embroidery thread:
   1 skein each Mauve 210, 333, 340;
   Green 472, 704, 905
White cotton lace edging, 2cm (¾in)
   wide and 75cm (30in) long
Small amount of terylene or polyester
   filling
Pot pourri
Very narrow lavender satin ribbon,
   80cm (31in) long
White and lavender sewing thread
Wooden frame, 20cm (8in) square

TO MAKE THE SCENTED SACHET
1 Mount the Fine Aida fabric on the frame, ensuring the straight grain of the fabric is parallel to the sides of the frame.
2 Find the centre of the fabric by counting the sets of threads. Mark with Basting Stitches horizontal and vertical centre guidelines to give the centre of

XXX XXX	333
XXX XXX	340
XXX XXX	210
XXX XXX	905
XXX XXX	704
XXX XXX	472

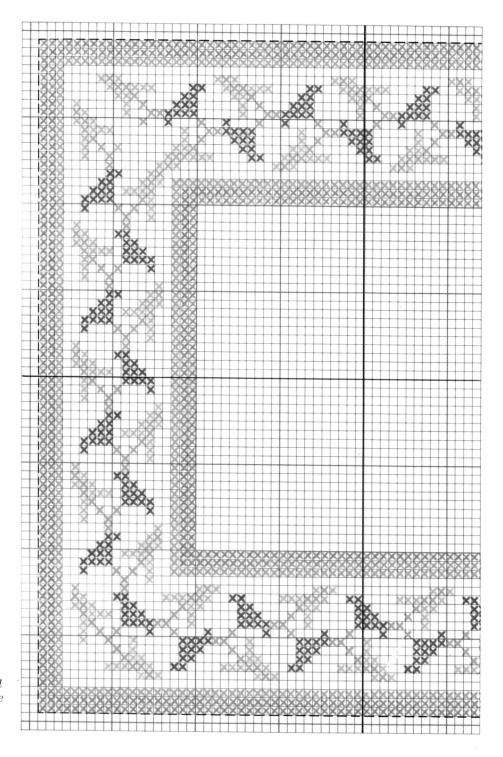

With experimentation this chart could also be used with thicker yarns and canvas to produce a beautiful cushion.

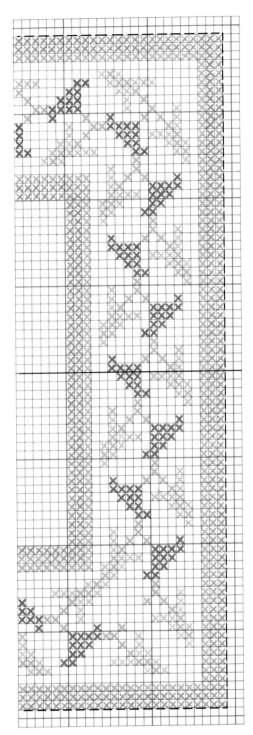

the fabric. This will also divide the working area into quarter sections.

3 Use *two* strands of thread at all times and follow the chart (see opposite) of the small stylized border pattern. Carefully and accurately work the three-colour bands and then the tiny flowers and leaves, using the appropriate threads. You will see that the two corners of the border design are not identical and that the opposite corners match each other. This is so the pattern fits together and 'flows' well.

4 Work the centre section of the sachet to match the square of the all-over design (see page 25), substituting the shades of pink for mauve.

5 When the stitchery is complete remove the fabric from the frame and cut away the surplus fabric, leaving a 1cm (⅜in) seam allowance on all sides.

6 With right sides facing, pin and baste the lace edging around the sachet on the seam line, folding and mitring the lace at the corners rather than gathering it. Then place the backing square face downwards over the embroidered fabric and baste the layers together.

7 With white sewing thread machine Straight Stitch around the sachet along the seam line. Leave a small opening along one side.

8 Carefully trim the surplus fabric across the corners of the seam allowance and turn the sachet to the right side and press gently.

9 Make a 14cm (5¼in) square lining bag, using the two squares of white cotton fabric. Place the polyester or terylene filling and the pot pourri inside the bag. Turn in the raw edges of the opening and neatly Slip Stitch the open sides together to close.

10 Place the lining bag carefully inside the sachet. Turn in the raw edges of the opening and with small Slip Stitches close the opening.

11 Finally, divide the narrow ribbon into four equal lengths. Thread a length of ribbon through the lace at each corner of the sachet and tie in a neat bow. Then, with matching thread, stitch through the knot of the bow to secure it permanently and complete the scented sachet, giving a neat finish.

CONVOLVULUS CANVASWORK CUSHION

This beautiful cushion is worked entirely in Cross Stitch on canvas and has been created by repeating the basic square of the repeat pattern in a staggered brick pattern (see chart and key on page 25).

MATERIALS

White mono canvas (15 holes per in), 56cm (22in) square
DMC tapisserie wool: 14 skeins Ecru; 7 skeins Green 7382; 5 skeins Green 7598; 3 skeins Pink 7135; 2 skeins each Green 7422, Pink 7133
Green fabric suitable to back cushion, 40cm (16in) square
Cushion pad, 38cm (15in) square
Sewing thread to match Green 7382
Basting thread
Wooden frame, 50cm (20in)
Waterproof marking pen

First the entwined design is worked and then the background is filled with ecru Cross Stitches to cover the canvas completely.

TO MAKE THE CUSHION

1 Stretch the canvas on the frame, ensuring the threads are parallel to the sides of the frame.

2 Using the waterproof marking pen, measure and then mark on the canvas a 38cm (15in) square. Then within this square carefully measure and mark out the grid pattern of the all-over repeat design. Each square of the chart represents one Cross Stitch, which in turn is worked over two horizontal and two vertical threads of canvas, so that each block of the repeat design equals forty Cross Stitches or eighty threads of canvas (see chart on page 25), and the blocks fit together in a brick wall pattern. Start at one side of your square on the canvas and work across, drawing in the vertical lines. Then add the staggered horizontal lines. This grid pattern will help you when you are working the Cross Stitches on the canvas as you will have guidelines to ensure you are following the design accurately.

3 Follow the chart using the colour key for tapisserie wools and remember to work your Cross Stitches so that all the upper stitches face the same way to produce an even effect. Do not use very long lengths of yarn as the action of passing the soft woollen yarn through the holes of the canvas will wear the yarn thin.

4 You will find it easier if you start by working the entwined stems as they will give you a good framework upon which to build the rest of the design. Once you have established the design on the canvas you can continue with any area you like. Do not jump across the wrong side of the canvas from one area to another without fastening the yarn as it will produce an untidy effect and waste yarn.

5 Once you have completed the entwined design fill in the background.

6 When the stitchery is complete remove the canvas from the frame and

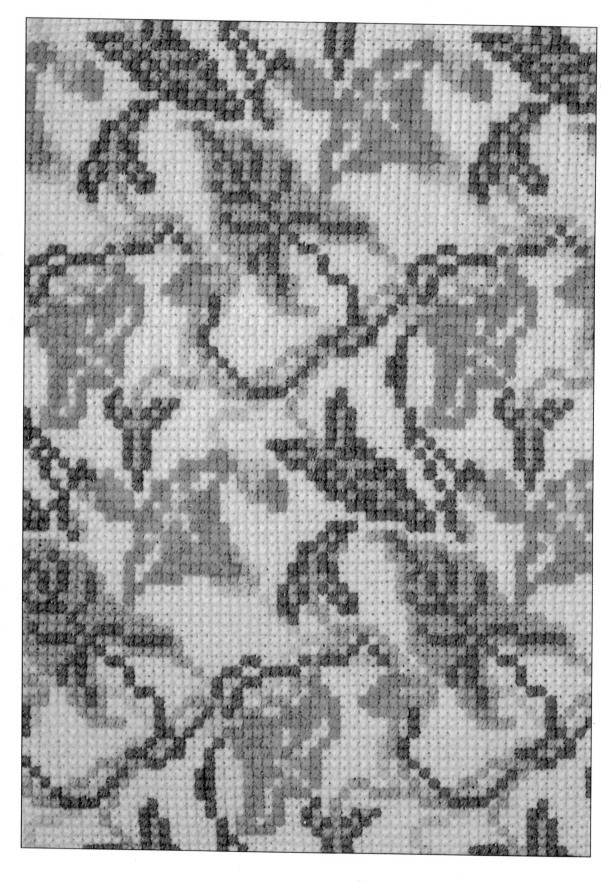

XXX XXX	7135
XXX XXX	7133
XXX XXX	Ecru
XXX XXX	7598
XXX XXX	7382
XXX XXX	7422

When repeated in the staggered pattern below, the square chart gives the all-over design of the canvaswork cushion.

trim the surplus canvas, leaving a 1cm (⅜in) seam allowance on all sides.

7 With the right sides facing, pin then baste and accurately machine Straight Stitch the cushion backing fabric to the canvaswork face along the edge of the canvaswork stitchery. Remember to leave an opening along one side to push the cushion pad in.

Carefully snip across the seam allowance at the corners and turn the cover to the right side. Fill with the cushion pad. Fold in the raw edges of the opening and with small Slip Stitches neatly hand sew the edges together to close.

8 Make four equal lengths of twisted cord as follows, using the two complete skeins of Green 7382. Carefully unravel each skein and cut in half. Then divide each half into three equal lengths. Use three lengths at a time to make four twisted cords (see Special Techniques, page 133). Tie a knot at each end of the cords and trim the excess yarn, teasing them out to form mock tassels.

9 Sew the cords evenly along the sides of the cushion using the green sewing thread to match Green 7382.

CORNFLOWER

*Today the cornflower is thought of as a
summer-flowering plant found in brilliant clumps in
cottage-style gardens. However, it is really
a wild flower which was once abundant in cornfields
and waste areas throughout the
countryside and was often considered to be a weed.*

CORNFLOWER
PICKLE OR JAM POT COVERS

These charming pot covers will enhance your jars of homemade pickles or jams and make very special gifts.

The size of the covers can easily be varied simply by using a different gauge of evenweave fabric. Use a fine fabric which will give small Cross Stitches for a small cover and a fabric which will give larger Cross Stitches for a larger cover.

MATERIALS

For the small cover (11cm [4½in] diameter):
Pearl Aida fabric (Zweigart E1007 colour Cream 264), 15cm (6in) square
Cream lace edging, 1cm (⅜in) wide and 38cm (15in) long
DMC stranded embroidery thread: small amounts Blue 798, 823; Green 320, 369, 992
Cream sewing thread

For the medium cover (20cm [8in] diameter):
Pearl Aida fabric (Zweigart E1007 colour Cream 264), 25cm (10in) square
Cream lace edging, 1cm (⅜in) wide and 70cm (28in) long
DMC stranded embroidery thread: 1 skein each Blue 341, 798, 823; Green 320, 369, 501
Cream sewing thread

For the large cover (26cm [10¼in] diameter):
Hertarette fabric (Zweigart E3707 colour Cream 264), 30cm (12in) square
Cream lace edging, 1cm (⅜in) wide and 85cm (34in) long
DMC soft embroidery cotton thread: 1 skein each Blue 2798, 2800; Black 2310; Green 2564, 2909, 2912
Cream sewing thread

You will also need embroidery hoops of a suitable size for each cover and lengths of satin ribbon 3mm (⅛in) wide to tie the covers on to the jars.

To Make the Covers

1 Choose which cover you want to make and place the appropriate piece of fabric centrally in the embroidery hoop. Mark with Basting Stitches the horizontal and vertical centre guidelines to establish the centre of the working area.

2 When working the small and medium covers use three strands of embroidery thread at all times. See point 5 if you are working the large cover. Remember to make all the upper stitches of the Cross Stitches face the same direction to achieve an even effect and work each Cross Stitch over one set of horizontal and vertical threads (the fabrics used will clearly show you the size of the stitch).

3 *The small cover* is suitable for a pot with a diameter of approximately 5cm (2in).

3a Carefully measure and mark with Basting Stitches an 11cm (4½in) diameter circle, using your centre point as the centre of the circle.

3b Work the starlike centre motif of four cornflowers, then work the tiny stylized flowers randomly around the centre motif and to within 6mm (¼in) of the perimeter line. Use Green 992 to work the single green Cross Stitches of these tiny flowers.

3c Once complete, remove the fabric from the hoop and trim away the surplus fabric, cutting around the line of Basting Stitches to give a circle. Pin and baste the cream lace edging around the edge of the lid cover and machine Zigzag Stitch the lace to the cover using cream sewing thread.

3d Hand stitch the cut ends of the lace together for a neat finish.

4 *The medium cover* is suitable for a pot with a diameter of approximately 8cm (3¼in).

4a Place the Pearl Aida fabric within the embroidery hoop and then find and mark with Basting Stitches the centre guidelines, as for the small cover.

Opposite, using different fabrics and yarns you can produce a variety of sizes of jam pot covers.

4b Work the central motif and then the border pattern. You will see the chart on page 31 gives a quarter section of the circular design so you will have to repeat this four times to give a complete circle.

4c Once your embroidery is complete remove the fabric from the hoop. Accurately measure and mark with Basting Stitches a circle measuring 20cm (8in) diameter. Cut away the surplus fabric

and complete with cream lace edging in the same way as for the small cover.

5 *The large cover* is suitable for a pot with a diameter of approximately 10cm (4in).

5a This is worked in the same way as the medium cover except that soft embroidery cotton thread is used on the larger gauge fabric to give a bolder effect.

5b Prepare, work and make up the cover as before, working to a finished size of 26cm (10¼in) diameter.

Tie each pickle or jam pot cover on to the jar using the lengths of narrow satin ribbon.

✗✗✗	798	✗✗✗	798	✗✗✗	2798
✗✗✗	823	✗✗✗	341	✗✗✗	2800
✗✗✗	369	✗✗✗	823	✗✗✗	2310
✗✗✗	992	✗✗✗	369	✗✗✗	2564
✗✗✗	320	✗✗✗	320	✗✗✗	2912
		✗✗✗	501	✗✗✗	2909

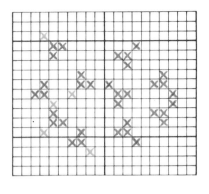

The chart above suggests how the random pattern can be built up. The larger chart gives a quarter segment of the border and centre design used for the box lid and pot covers.

The keys given are, left to right, for the small, medium and large covers.

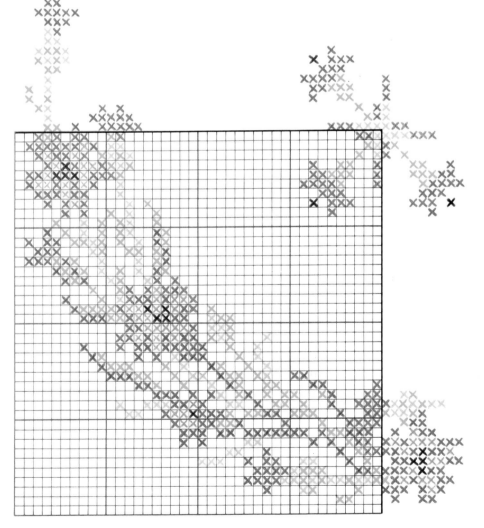

Overleaf, *you can see the versatility of the cornflower design as it is used to decorate the jars of pickle and also the charming box.*

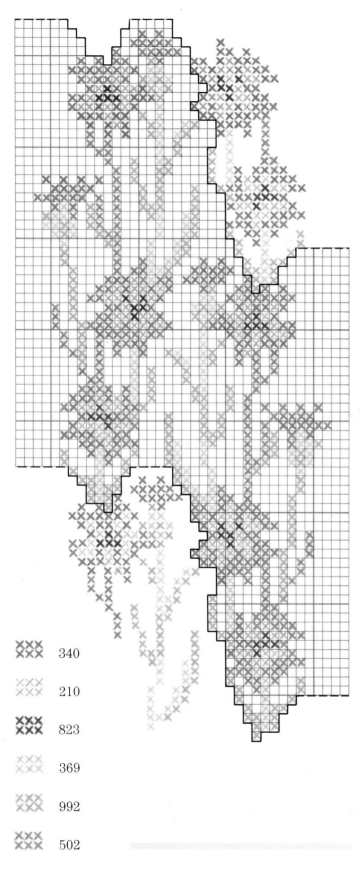

340	
210	
823	
369	
992	
502	

CORNFLOWER EMBROIDERED BOX

This beautiful box can be used to hold hankies, jewellery or cosmetics and will enhance your dressing table. It is made quite simply by working the circular design of the pickle or jam pot cover although it has the tiny random flowers worked in the middle of the design instead of the centre motif. Then a long strip of the linear repeat pattern is worked around the sides of the box.

The repeat pattern of the sides could also be used to make a delightful border for bath linen or, if it is repeated widthways as well as lengthways, it will become an all-over design suitable for a cushion worked on canvas.

MATERIALS

Pearl Aida fabric (Zweigart E1007 colour Cream 264), 50 × 70cm (20 × 28in)
Pelmet weight interfacing (Vilene), 40 × 80cm (16 × 31in)
Printed cotton fabric suitable for lining box, 35 × 65cm (14 × 25½in)
Thin flexible white cardboard, 30 × 60cm (12 × 23½in)
DMC stranded embroidery thread: 2 skeins each Blue 340; Green 992; 1 skein each Mauve 210; Green 369, 502; Blue 823
DMC coton perlé No.5 thread: 1 skein each Green 992; Mauve 210
Sewing thread to match Mauve 210
Cream sewing thread
Basting thread
Wooden embroidery hoops, 15cm (6in) diameter and 20cm (8in) diameter
Sharp craft knife to cut cardboard

TO MAKE THE BOX

1 Accurately cut out the evenweave fabric, interfacing, lining fabric and cardboard, following the cutting guide on page 35.

2 Stretch the square piece of even-weave fabric centrally in the larger hoop. This will become the lid of the box.

3 Mark with Basting Stitches the horizontal and vertical centre guidelines to establish the centre of the fabric. This will also divide the fabric within the hoop into quarter sections.

4 Use three strands of thread at all times and work your Cross Stitches so that all the upper stitches face the same direction to achieve an even effect. Work each Cross Stitch over one set of horizontal and vertical threads.

5 Carefully follow the chart on page 31 of the quarter section of the circular design. Count outwards from the centre to establish accurately where to start the stitchery. Repeat the quarter section until the design is complete. Then work the tiny stylized flowers to give a random pattern within the circular design using Green 992 to complete the flower motifs.

6 Remove the fabric from the hoop and press it gently on the wrong side with a steam iron to remove any creases and encourage the stitchery to appear embossed.

7 Work the linear repeat pattern along the centre of the long strip of Pearl Aida fabric. Place one end of the fabric strip in the small hoop (you will have to reposition the hoop several times along the strip). Work your repeat pattern by stitching from the top of the chart and working downwards repeating the pattern as necessary. (The black stepped line shows you where the repeat pattern starts and finishes and how it fits together.) Work along the strip until you have worked 61cm (24in) of the design. Remove the fabric from the hoop and press it gently on the wrong side to encourage an embossed effect.

8 To make the box, place the long, embroidered strip face downwards on a clean, flat surface. Place one of the interfacing strips over it so that the embroidery is centrally positioned. Pin to hold, then trim away the surplus fabric leaving a 1cm (⅜in) turning allowance on all sides of the embroidery. Turn this allowance over the edge of

CUTTING PLAN FOR CORNFLOWER EMBROIDERED BOX

CREAM PEARL AIDA FABRIC

25cm (10in)
25cm (10in)
21cm (8¼in)
50cm (20in)
70cm (28in)
20cm (8in)
70cm (28in)

PELMET-WEIGHT 'VILENE' INTERFACING

9cm (3½in) 60cm (23½in)
19cm (7½in) 19cm (7½in) 19cm (7½in) 19cm (7½in)
40cm (16in)
9cm (3½in) 60cm (23½in)
80cm (31in)

COTTON PRINT LINING FABRIC

21cm (8¼in) 21cm (8¼in)
35cm (14in)
62cm (24½in)
11cm (4½in)
65cm (25½in)

THIN FLEXIBLE CARDBOARD

19cm (7½in) 19cm (7½in)
30cm (12in)
9cm (3½in) 60cm (23½in)
60cm (23½in)

Trim cardboard shapes very slightly to make them slightly smaller than interfacing shapes.

the interfacing strip and baste to hold, taking care not to stitch through the fabric layers to the embroidered face of the strip as these stitches can stay in position permanently. Repeat this step with the strip of print fabric and the remaining piece of interfacing.

9 Similarly cover one of the interfacing circles with the embroidered circular design, centring it carefully and trimming away the surplus fabric, leaving a 1cm (⅜in) turning allowance on the embroidery. Turn this allowance over and baste to hold, as in step 8. Then use the remaining circles of Pearl Aida and cotton print to cover the three remaining interfacing circles.

10 With right sides facing outwards, pin one of the print fabric circles to the embroidered lid circle and with a double length of cream sewing thread Slip Stitch the edges together. Place a cardboard circle in between the two layers of the lid before stitching all round the edges. Slip Stitch neatly but in any case this join will be covered by a twisted cord.

11 Similarly Slip Stitch the Pearl Aida base circle and the remaining lining

circle together with a cardboard circle in between the layers.

12 Stitch the lining strip to the base circle, using a double length of cream thread and remembering to have the print lining of the base and the side strip facing into the box. Stitch the short ends of the strip together to give the back seam.

13 Then, matching the short ends of the embroidered strip with those of the lining, stitch the strips together. Start by stitching around the top or rim of the box sides so that you are stitching through the edge of the embroidered fabric and the print fabric. Then join the short side ends of the embroidered fabric together. Carefully ease the strip of cardboard into position between the layers of the sides before stitching the lower edges of the sides to the base.

14 Make two lengths of twisted cord using the mauve and green coton perlé thread. For each cord cut a 4m (4⅜yd) length of each colour. Fold each cut length equally into four strands but do not cut them. Then use the four strands of green and the four strands of mauve to make a two-colour cord (see Special Techniques page 133). Repeat to make a second length of cord.

15 Using mauve sewing thread sew one cord around the edge of the box lid tying the surplus cord ends evenly into a neat bow; stitch the knot of the bow to hold it in position. Make mock tassels at the ends of the cord by knotting the cord near to the ends and teasing out the cut threads.

16 Stitch the second length of cord around the edge of the base of the box, beginning and ending at the back seam line. You will need to trim the excess cord and oversew the raw end very neatly to prevent the cord from unravelling and fraying.

17 Place the lid on to the top of the open box, ensuring that the small bow is positioned at the front and is directly opposite the back seam line of the box. With double thread for extra strength Slip Stitch the lid to the edge of the back of the box, stitching 2cm (¾in) along the edge on either side of the seamline to complete this pretty box.

The central area of the cornflower box has the random pattern of tiny stylized flowers to link with the box sides.

FIELD POPPY

The field or common poppy, with its
brilliant red petals that bring rich splashes of colour
to cornfields, waste ground and hedgerows
throughout the country, has been used as the design
source of this cushion and
the accompanying pretty gift cards.

XXX XXX	900
XXX XXX	947
XXX XXX	971
XXX XXX	732
XXX XXX	907
XXX XXX	369
XXX XXX	315
XXX XXX	310
XXX XXX	613
XXX XXX	676

For the yellow version of this card use the thread numbers given below.

XXX XXX	972
XXX XXX	726
XXX XXX	307
XXX XXX	732
XXX XXX	907
XXX XXX	369
XXX XXX	734
XXX XXX	704
XXX XXX	613
XXX XXX	676

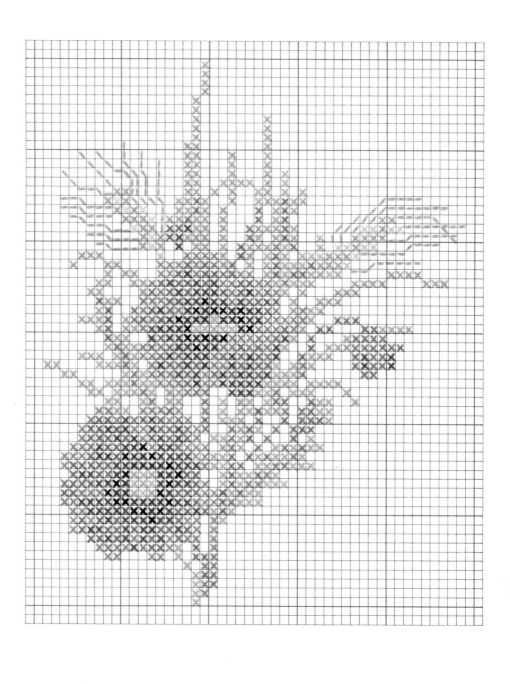

FIELD POPPY GIFT CARDS

These charming cards using variations of colour would make very special gifts as, once given, they can be framed to make beautiful wall pictures.

The motif for the cards (see the chart on the left) has been extracted from the quarter section which is used for the circular design of the cushion (see page 45). They are worked in different colours to give the yellow Welsh poppy and an orange-red variation of the field poppy. If you look carefully at the chart on pages 44–5 you will be able to recognise which part of the cushion design has been used.

To complete the motif extend the poppy stems freely and add some barley stalks to the base of the design to achieve a more balanced effect.

MATERIALS
(For each card)
White Hardanger fabric (Zweigart E1008), 25 × 30cm (10 × 12in)
Very thin card (cream or other suitable colour), 24 × 51cm (9½ × 20in)
Clear adhesive glue suitable for fabric and card
DMC stranded embroidery thread (small amounts only):
 Yellow poppies: Yellow 307, 676, 726, 972; Green 369, 704, 732, 734, 907; Brown 613
 Orange-red poppies: Black 310; Brown 315, 613; Green 369, 732, 907; Yellow 676; Orange 900, 947, 971
Small rectangular embroidery frame

To MAKE THE GIFT CARDS
1 Mount the fabric on the frame ensuring the straight grain is parallel to the sides of the frame.
2 Find and mark with Basting Stitch the horizontal and vertical centre guidelines to find the centre of the fabric.
3 Use the colour key of your chosen poppy variation and the chart on the left to work the design. Use three strands of embroidery thread and work each Cross Stitch over two vertical and two horizontal threads of the fabric. Make all the upper stitches of the Cross Stitches face the same way in order to achieve an even effect. Remember to extend the lower stems of the poppies and barley.
4 When the stitchery is complete remove the fabric from the frame and press it gently on the wrong side with a steam iron, if necessary.
5 Make the gift card by lightly marking the thin card to divide it into three equal rectangles. Within the middle section measure and draw in the centre a small rectangle measuring 12 × 18cm (4¾ × 7¼in). Use a sharp craft knife to cut this out. If you wish, you can position the window cut-out slightly towards the top of the card rather than exactly in the centre to give a pleasing effect. (See Special Techniques, page 133.)
6 Trim away the excess fabric around the embroidered poppy motif ensuring you leave a border large enough to overlap the edges of the cut-out window. (Trim a little fabric away at a time until you achieve the correct size.)
7 Carefully place the design behind the 'frame' of the gift card and use the clear adhesive glue to hold it centrally within the cut-out frame. Then fold the backing section over the wrong side of the design and glue them together to complete the gift card.

Overleaf, *the brilliant red poppies stand out against the muted colours of the ripening cornfield.*

✖✖✖ ✖✖✖	817
✖✖✖ ✖✖✖	606
✖✖✖ ✖✖✖	351
✖✖✖ ✖✖✖	732
✖✖✖ ✖✖✖	907
✖✖✖ ✖✖✖	472
✖✖✖ ✖✖✖	315
✖✖✖ ✖✖✖	310
✖✖✖ ✖✖✖	729
✖✖✖ ✖✖✖	745

The chart shows a quarter segment of the circular design to make up the Field Poppy cushion.

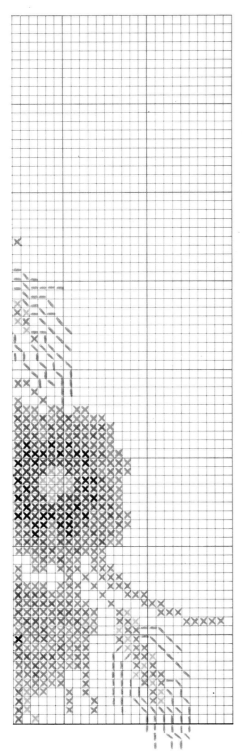

FIELD POPPY CUSHION

The cushion design is achieved by repeating the quarter section given in the chart on the left. Stems of barley have been introduced into the design to complement the strong colours of the poppies.

It is worked on Hardanger fabric but could easily be worked on other even-weave fabrics or canvas to alter the scale of the design. For example, it could be worked in rug wools on canvas to create a beautiful circular rug.

MATERIALS
Ecru Hardanger fabric (Zweigart E1008) 56cm (22in) square
Ecru fabric suitable for backing the cushion, 43cm (17in) square
DMC stranded embroidery threads:
    2 skeins each Red 351; Yellow 729;
    1 skein each Black 310; Brown 315;
    Green 472, 732, 907; Red 606, 817;
    Yellow 745
DMC coton perlé No.5 threads: 1 skein each Red 606; Green 732
Cushion pad, 40cm (16in) square
Ecru and red sewing thread
Basting thread
Embroidery frame, 50cm (20in) square

TO WORK THE CIRCULAR POPPY DESIGN
1 Mount the Hardanger fabric on the frame ensuring the grain of the fabric is straight and the threads are parallel to the sides of the frame.
2 Find and mark with Basting Stitches the horizontal and vertical centre guide-lines to give the centre where your basting stitches intersect. This will also divide the working area into quarters.
3 Carefully count outwards along one of the guidelines to the point where you wish to commence stitching. (You will find it advisable to start with the stems of the poppies that intersect the guide-lines, rather than the stalks of barley, as the poppy stems will lead you more clearly into the design.)

This design would look equally effective if made into a circular cushion.

4 Work each Cross Stitch over two horizontal and two vertical sets of threads of the fabric and use three strands of embroidery thread at all times. Remember that all the upper stitches of the Cross Stitches must face the same direction to achieve a smooth and effective result.

5 Work around the circular design repeating the quarter section four times, working neatly and economically on the wrong side of the fabric, without jumping from one area of the design to another with your thread.

6 Once your poppy circle is complete remove the fabric from the frame. Gently press the wrong side of the fabric with a steam iron to encourage an embossed effect. On the wrong side, with the aid of the horizontal and vertical guidelines, measure and mark (with dressmakers' pins) a 40cm (16in) square, which becomes the seam line, with the poppy circle centred within the square.

7 Make up the cushion. With right sides facing pin, baste and machine Straight Stitch the Hardanger fabric and backing fabric together using the ecru sewing thread and leaving a 1cm (⅜in) seam allowance. Remember to leave an opening along one side large enough to insert the cushion pad. Turn the cushion to the right side.

8 Place the cushion pad in position and neatly Slip Stitch the folded edges of the opening together using ecru thread.

9 Make a green and red twisted cord to link with the bright colours of the poppy design, using the skeins of coton perlé thread. Divide each skein into four equal lengths (see Special Techniques, page 133).

10 Starting at one corner, attach the cord to the cushion using red sewing thread and small Slip Stitches, leaving approximately 10cm (4in) of cord hanging at the first corner. Then, when you reach this corner again, having attached the cord right around the cushion, trim the excess cord to leave a similar length, knotting the cord before you cut it to prevent it untwisting. Finally, tie and stitch the ends into a small bow and tease out the loose ends.

DAISY

The daisy is often regarded as a common weed since it grows abundantly, both in the wild and in well-tended garden lawns. It has been gathered and made into daisy chains by the young as well as being celebrated in poetry, and even used in herbal remedies.

CUTTING PLAN FOR DAISY HEXAGONAL BOX

EVENWEAVE FABRIC

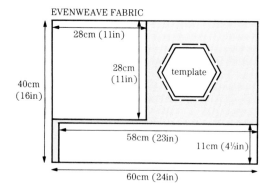

HEAVYWEIGHT INTERFACING

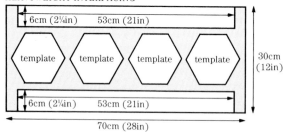

PRINT COTTON LINING FABRIC

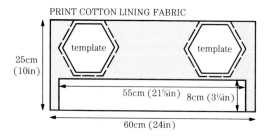

CARDBOARD

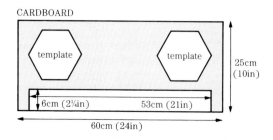

The broken line outside the template shape indicates 1cm (⅜in) turning allowance to be added.

DAISY HEXAGONAL BOX

This brightly coloured box has its stitchery worked upon a fine evenweave fabric of sage green colour to give a rich feeling. The lid is created by working six daisy plant motifs evenly around a centre point, while the sides of the box are worked as a single strip of stylized flowers and leaves creating a jewelled effect.

MATERIALS

'Linda' fabric (Zweigart E1235 colour 603 Sage), 40 × 60cm (16 × 24in)

Pelmet weight interfacing (Vilene), 30 × 70cm (12 × 28in)

Printed cotton fabric suitable to line the box, 25 × 60cm (10 × 24in)

Cardboard (thick enough to give firm shape to sides), 25 × 60cm (10 × 24in)

DMC stranded embroidery thread: 1 skein each Yellow 444; Orange 742; White; Pink 335, 605, 819; Green 472, 469, 907

DMC coton perlé thread No.5: 1 skein each Pink 605; Green 907

Sewing thread to match sage-coloured fabric

Sewing thread to match either skein of coton perlé thread

Basting thread

Strong adhesive glue suitable for cardboard and fabric

Wooden embroidery hoop, 10cm (4in) in diameter

Wooden embroidery hoop, 20cm (8in) in diameter

Sharp craft knife to cut cardboard

TO MAKE HEXAGONAL BOX

1 Using the cutting plan on the left, accurately cut out all the shapes of fabric, interfacing and cardboard. (Use the template of the hexagon opposite to cut out the lid and base pieces, remem-

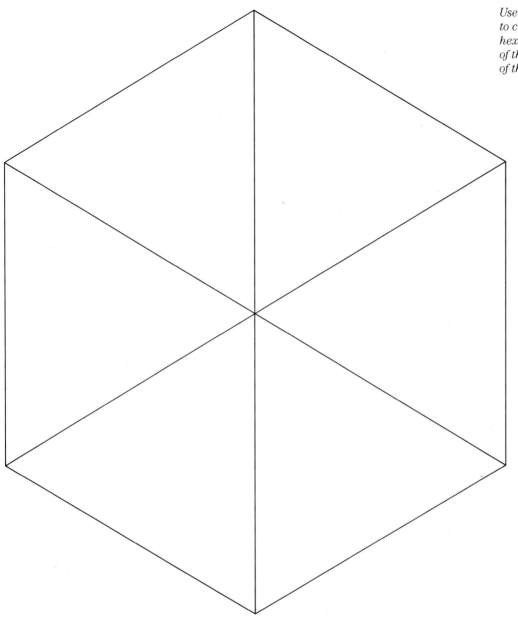

Use this template to cut out the hexagonal shapes of the lid and base of the box.

bering to allow 1cm (⅜in) turning allowance where indicated.) Carefully use the craft knife to cut out the cardboard shapes on a cutting board.

2 Put all the cut shapes to one side and place the 28cm (11in) square of even-weave fabric centrally within the larger embroidery hoop. Mark with Basting Stitches the horizontal and vertical centre guidelines to establish the centre of the working area within the hoop. Note that these lines intersect in the middle of a square on the chart. When working your embroidery each Cross Stitch is worked over two horizontal and two vertical threads of fabric, so that the centre square of the chart is the equivalent to a central Cross Stitch of the embroidery.

3 Use three strands of embroidery thread at all times and remember to make all the upper stitches of the Cross Stitches face the same direction to achieve an even effect. Working from

the chart on page 55, count outwards from the centre along one of the guidelines to locate a starting point and carefully follow the chart to work the daisy design.

4 Work the six daisy plant motifs to complete the embroidery for the hexagonal box lid. Remove the fabric from the hoop and press it gently with a steam iron, on the wrong side, to encourage an embossed effect.

5 Cut out a hexagonal template using tracing paper. Draw three lines connecting each corner with the corner directly opposite to divide the hexagon into triangles. Place this template over the right side of the embroidered lid design, making sure that the centres of each align and adjusting the position until each daisy motif is balanced within each triangular shape. Pin the paper template in position, then trim the fabric around its edges, adding a 1cm (⅜in) turning allowance all round. Leave the paper template pinned to the fabric.

6 Work the embroidered strip to go around the six sides of the box in the following way. Mark with the Basting Stitches an area centrally within the strip of evenweave fabric, to measure 6 × 53cm (2¼ × 21 in). (You can use one of the interfacing strips to help you do this.)

7 Place one end of the strip within the smaller hoop and work the random pattern of tiny flowers along the strip, working within the basted shape (see page 55, top) and repositioning the hoop as necessary. You will find it easier to work the centres of the flowers first, spacing them evenly along the strip and balancing the use of yellow and orange. Then work the four Cross Stitch petals around the centres and finally work the two Cross Stitch leaves. Remember your aim is to achieve a random pattern as if the flowers have been scattered along the strip.

8 Once this is complete remove the fabric from the hoop and press it gently on the wrong side, using a steam iron. This will encourage the stitchery to have an embossed effect. Trim away the excess fabric remembering to leave a turning allowance of 1cm (⅜in) all round.

9 Make the box as follows. With the tracing paper template still pinned to the right side of the lid, place an interfacing hexagon underneath the embroidered fabric so that it matches the position of the paper template. Fold the turning allowance of the evenweave fabric over the edges of the interfacing hexagon and baste to hold in position. Take care to fold the corners accurately and do not stitch right through the embroidered side of the fabric as the basting can then remain permanently in place. Remove the paper template.

10 Cover the other three interfacing hexagons with the two cotton lining fabric shapes and the evenweave fabric shape in the same way.

11 Trim a little from each side of the cardboard hexagons, so that they are slightly smaller than the fabric-covered hexagons.

12 Using a double length of green thread to match the evenweave fabric, sew the embroidered lid and a lining shape together (with right sides outside), sandwiching a cardboard shape between the two layers. Use very small, neat stitches. Similarly sandwich the other cardboard hexagon in between the evenweave base and lining shapes, stitching these layers together.

13 Cover one of the long interfacing strips with the lining fabric, turning the fabric over the edges of the strip and basting to hold it in position (do not stitch through to the right side). Leave one short end free so that you can adjust the length of the covered strip when you stitch it in place to the base of the box.

14 Cover the other interfacing strip with the embroidered evenweave fabric, matching the area of stitchery with the interfacing shape. Once more, leave one short end free for later adjustment.

15 With the lining side of the base facing upwards, stitch the lining strip around the edges of the hexagonal shape. Use a double length of green thread and work small, neat stitches, starting and ending at one of the corner points to give a better finish.

The bright pinks, yellow and orange stand out richly against the green fabric to bring this design to life.

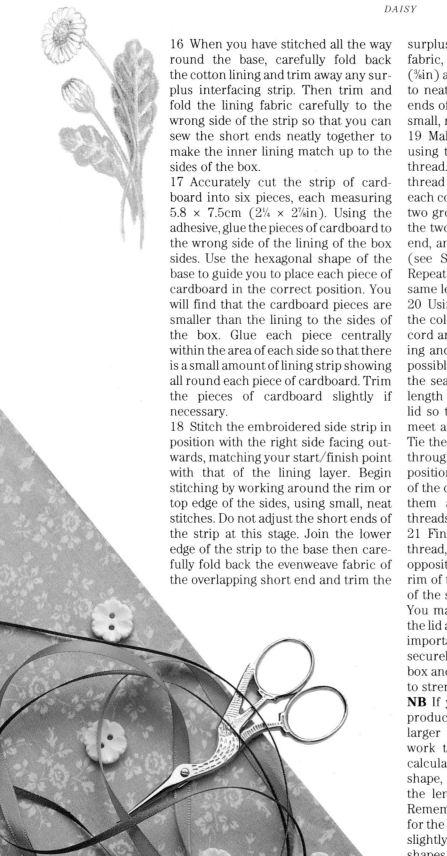

16 When you have stitched all the way round the base, carefully fold back the cotton lining and trim away any surplus interfacing strip. Then trim and fold the lining fabric carefully to the wrong side of the strip so that you can sew the short ends neatly together to make the inner lining match up to the sides of the box.

17 Accurately cut the strip of cardboard into six pieces, each measuring 5.8 × 7.5cm (2¼ × 2⅞in). Using the adhesive, glue the pieces of cardboard to the wrong side of the lining of the box sides. Use the hexagonal shape of the base to guide you to place each piece of cardboard in the correct position. You will find that the cardboard pieces are smaller than the lining to the sides of the box. Glue each piece centrally within the area of each side so that there is a small amount of lining strip showing all round each piece of cardboard. Trim the pieces of cardboard slightly if necessary.

18 Stitch the embroidered side strip in position with the right side facing outwards, matching your start/finish point with that of the lining layer. Begin stitching by working around the rim or top edge of the sides, using small, neat stitches. Do not adjust the short ends of the strip at this stage. Join the lower edge of the strip to the base then carefully fold back the evenweave fabric of the overlapping short end and trim the surplus interfacing. Trim the evenweave fabric, remembering to leave the 1cm (⅜in) allowance. Tuck this allowance in to neaten and then sew the two short ends of evenweave fabric together with small, neat stitches.

19 Make two lengths of twisted cord, using the pink and green coton perlé thread. Cut a 4m (4⅜yd) length of pink thread and also of green thread. Fold each colour in half and half again giving two groups of four threads each. Knot the two sets of colours together at one end, and use to make the twisted cord (see Special Techniques, page 133). Repeat to make a second cord of the same length.

20 Using sewing thread to match one of the colours of the cord, Slip Stitch one cord around the base of the box, starting and finishing the cord as neatly as possible at the same corner of the box as the seam. Then Slip Stitch the second length of cord around the edges of the lid so that equal amounts of the cord meet at the centre of one of the sides. Tie the ends into a neat bow and stitch through the knot to hold it securely in position. Make mock tassels at the ends of the cord by knotting them, trimming them and teasing out the trimmed threads carefully.

21 Finally, with a double length of thread, sew the edge of the lid that lies opposite to the one with the bow to the rim of the box, so that the seam or join of the sides lies at the back of the box. You may find it quite awkward to hold the lid and box whilst doing this, but it is important that you join them very securely. Work from the inside of the box and sew along the joined edge twice to strengthen it.

NB If you wish to use a fabric which produces larger Cross Stitches giving a larger overall design you will have to work the lid design first in order to calculate the size of the hexagonal shape, and from this you can measure the length of the strip for the sides. Remember that your cardboard shapes for the lid base and sides must always be slightly smaller than the interfacing shapes to allow for the thickness of the cardboard.

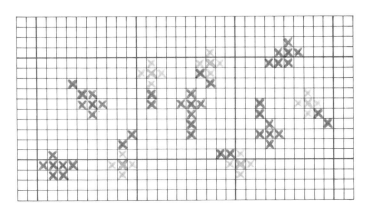

✕✕✕	444	✕✕✕	335
✕✕✕	742	✕✕✕	472
✕✕✕	White	✕✕✕	907
✕✕✕	819	✕✕✕	469
✕✕✕	605		

DAISY SEWING BASKET

A picnic basket lined with fabric and an embroidered design inside the lid will make a very attractive sewing basket.

This particular basket measures 26cm (10¼in) wide, 20cm (8in) deep and 13cm (5in) high and the materials and instructions refer to this size. Your own fabric requirements will obviously vary should you choose to use a larger or smaller basket.

If you wish to add matching accessories to your sewing basket work a single box shape with a daisy plant within it on the same pink Ainring fabric. Then trim around the edges of the embroidered area and make into a small pin cushion, backing it with either the same fabric or the pink striped fabric. Add a green ribbon tied in a neat bow at the centre of the top edge. Fill the pin cushion firmly.

Similarly, you could work another single box motif and use this to make the cover of a needlecase.

MATERIALS
Ainring fabric (Zweigart E3793 colour 414 Pink), 30 × 35cm (12 × 14in)
Pink and white striped cotton fabric, 40 × 90cm (16 × 36in)
Pelmet weight interfacing (Vilene), 26 × 40cm (10¼ × 16in)
Bright green satin ribbon, 3mm (⅛in) wide and 1.60m (1¾yd) long
DMC coton perlé No.5 thread: 1 skein each Green 369, 704, 992; Orange 741; Yellow 444; White; Pink 818, 957, 891; Brown 301
Sewing threads to match pink striped fabric and green ribbon
Basting thread
Transparent nylon thread
Tracing paper to make paper pattern
Suitable oblong frame

TO MAKE THE BASKET LINING
1 Work the embroidery for the lid as follows. Mount the evenweave fabric on the frame, making sure that the straight grain of the fabric is parallel to the sides of the frame to avoid distortion.

2. Using tracing paper, carefully make a paper pattern of the inside shape and size of the lid then cut this shape out of the paper. Place your paper pattern over the stretched evenweave fabric aligning the straight grain with the sides of the paper pattern. (You may not be able to do this on all four sides as sometimes the baskets are not exactly regular in shape.) Pin the pattern to the fabric and baste around the shape. Remove the paper pattern and keep it to one side (see step 6, where it is used again).

3 Referring to the daisy design chart on page 58 and also the diagram on page 59, you will see that the design is worked diagonally across the area of fabric which will become the lining of the lid. It does not really matter where you start working the grid pattern of the design, but it is advisable to work the continuous lines that run from the top right to the lower left first and then to work the staggered lines that complete the grid pattern and make the small boxes. Each individual box within the grid framework measures twenty-four Cross Stitches by twenty Cross Stitches. Work the grid of the design completely before beginning to work the daisy plant motifs within the grid.

4 Use a single length of coton perlé thread, remembering not to use a very long length of this yarn as it tends to wear thin and lose its sheen. Work all the Cross Stitches so that the upper stitches all face the same direction to give an even effect. Each Cross Stitch is worked over two horizontal sets and two vertical sets of threads of the Ainring fabric.

Work one line of daisy plants facing downwards and then work the next line facing upwards (see the photograph on the page opposite).

5 Once you have worked the daisy design over the area of the lid shape remove the fabric from the frame, trim away the surplus around the line of basting, allowing 1cm (⅜in) turning allowance all around. Press the fabric

This small picnic basket when opened reveals a beautifully embroidered lid and matching pin cushion and needlecase.

gently on the wrong side with a steam iron to encourage the embroidery to stand out with an embossed effect.

6 Using the paper pattern of the lid, cut out a lid shape from half of the heavy-weight interfacing. Pin this to the wrong side of the embroidered evenweave fabric, matching the cut shape to the basted line of the Cross Stitch design and baste the turning allowance of the evenweave fabric over the edge of the interfacing. Do not make your Basting Stitches go through to the right side of the evenweave fabric so that you can leave them permanently in position.

7 Pin the embroidered lining inside the basket lid. Using a double length of the transparent nylon thread for extra strength, carefully stitch the lining to the basket. You will have to make small stabbing stitches through the edge of

the lining shape, then through the woven pattern of the basket in order to ensure the lining is fixed securely in position.

8 Line the basket as follows. Referring to the cutting plan given on the right as guidance, carefully cut out the base, sides and pockets using the pink and white striped cotton fabric.

All measurements given refer to the size of basket shown in the photograph. If the basket you have chosen to make is larger or smaller then make a paper pattern of the inside base and sides, revising the pocket size if necessary, and then calculate the size of pieces of fabric that you will need to line it.

9 Make a paper pattern of the inside base and use this to cut out the base shape using the interfacing. Place this interfacing shape centrally over the wrong side of the striped fabric base.

992
704
369
444
741
301
891
957
818
White

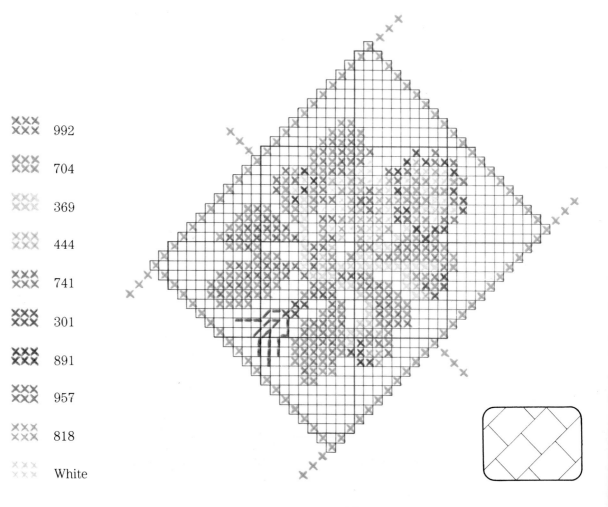

Cutting Plan for Daisy Sewing Basket

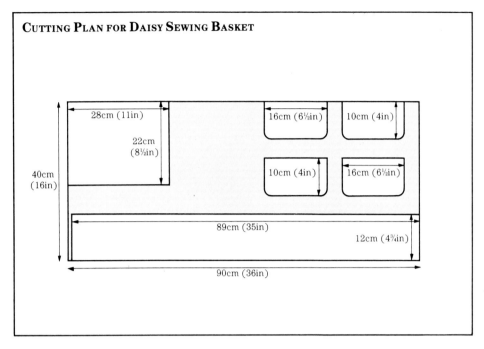

Using Straight Stitch and matching thread, machine around the interfacing shape, stitching as close to the edge as possible and attaching the interfacing to the striped fabric.

10 Using the cut edge of the interfacing as a guide to the exact shape of the base, pin and baste the striped fabric side strip to the striped base fabric, with right sides together. Before machining around this line, join the short ends of the strip where they meet.

11 Place the fabric lining inside the basket. Turn down the top edge of the fabric to the wrong side, to just below the edge of the basket, and pin around the turned edge to hold. Remove the lining from the basket and carefully machine using Straight Stitch close to the turned edge.

12 Make the pockets as follows. Turn and baste to the wrong side a 1cm (⅜in) turning allowance around the sides and base of the pocket shapes. Turn 6mm (¼in) to the wrong side along the top straight edge of each pocket, then fold 1.5cm (⅝in) to the wrong side and baste to hold.

13 Divide the bright green ribbon equally into four lengths and, using a wide Zigzag Stitch with green thread, appliqué the ribbon to the straight top edge of each pocket (make the Zigzag Stitching coincide with the hem on the wrong side of the top of the pocket).

The Zigzag Stitches will hold the ribbon in place but should not pass through the ribbon. Allow 1cm (⅜in) of ribbon to overlap at each side of the pocket and turn this over the edge and pin to hold in position. Then carefully draw the excess ribbon up and out at the centre of the pocket. Cut the loop of excess ribbon evenly in half at the centre and tie the ends into a neat bow. Stitch through the knot of the bow to secure it.

14 With the lining in position inside the basket, pin one pocket centrally on each of the four sides. The top of each pocket should be 1cm (⅜in) below the top edge of the basket lining.

15 Remove the lining from the basket once more and baste each pocket in position, then machine Straight Stitch down the sides and around the base of each pocket.

16 Replace the lining in the basket, arranging it in the correct position. Then, using the transparent nylon thread, stitch around the top edge of the lining to just below the top edge of the basket in the same way as you attached the embroidered lining to the basket lid.

PRIMROSE AND FORGET-ME-NOT

*The first flowering of the primrose in its
natural habitat is always welcome.
The romantically named forget-me-not is a cheerful
sight because of the early appearance of
its daintily shaped blue and pinkish flowers.*

PRIMROSE AND FORGET-ME-NOT TRAY CLOTH AND NAPKIN

Afternoon tea becomes a special occasion when served on a tray with this dainty tray cloth and pretty matching napkin.

The simple motif of primroses and forget-me-nots would look equally effective if worked on smaller place mats, along the border of guest towels or singly on greetings cards.

MATERIALS
For the tray cloth:
Pale green evenweave 'Linda' fabric (Zweigart E1235 colour eau-de-Nil 760), 45 × 55 cm (18 × 21½in)
For the napkin:
Pale green evenweave 'Linda' fabric (Zweigart E1235 colour eau-de-Nil 760), 45cm (18in) square
DMC stranded embroidery thread:
    1 skein each Green 561, 734, 904, 907, 992; Yellow 307, 445, 725, 972; Blue 519, 809; Pink 761
Blue sewing thread to match Blue 809
Basting thread
Embroidery hoop, 18cm (7in) in diameter

TO MAKE THE TRAY CLOTH
1 Accurately measure and mark with Basting Stitch a rectangle measuring 35 × 46cm (14 × 18in) centrally within the larger piece of evenweave fabric. Baste a guideline 1cm (⅜in) inside both short ends of the tray cloth shape. Then baste another guideline thirty-two Cross Stitches in from the first (each Cross Stitch is worked over two horizontal and two vertical threads of fabric) to give you the two border strip areas within which the flower sprigs are worked.
2 Count the threads of the length of the border strip to find the midway point and match this to the midway point of the length of the motif.

3 Place the fabric area to be worked within the embroidery hoop. Begin stitching with the darker green of the forget-me-not foliage (Green 561) as this colour establishes the position of the flowers, stems and so on.

4 Work the motif and then reposition the hoop and repeat the motif above and below the central sprig of flowers leaving a space of four threads between each motif. Repeat this border at the opposite end of the tray cloth within the guidelines.

5 When the stitchery is complete press the fabric carefully on the wrong side with a steam iron to remove any creases.

6 Set your sewing machine to produce a decorative edging stitch and, using blue sewing thread, machine stitch around the tray cloth shape just on the inside of the Basting Stitches. If you wish you can carefully make the corners curved.

7 Then remove all basting thread and cut away the excess fabric with a pair of sharp-pointed trimming scissors.

8 Press once more if necessary. Spray starch may be used to produce a crisp effect.

To Make the Napkin

1 Measure and then mark out with Basting Stitches a 38cm (15in) square centrally within the remaining piece of evenweave fabric, to give the shape and size of the napkin.

2 Use the chart for the tray cloth (see right).

3 Place the top right corner of the fabric in the hoop and work a single motif of primroses and forget-me-nots, positioning the motif at least 1cm (⅜in) inside the basted guidelines.

4 Work the decorative edging in the same way as for the tray cloth (follow steps 5 to 8 of the instructions for the tray cloth).

NB If your sewing machine does not have the facility to work a decorative edging stitch, you can either work Satin Stitch around the edge or trim the excess fabric leaving a 1cm (⅜in) allowance which can then be turned to the wrong side and neatly hemmed either by hand or machine.

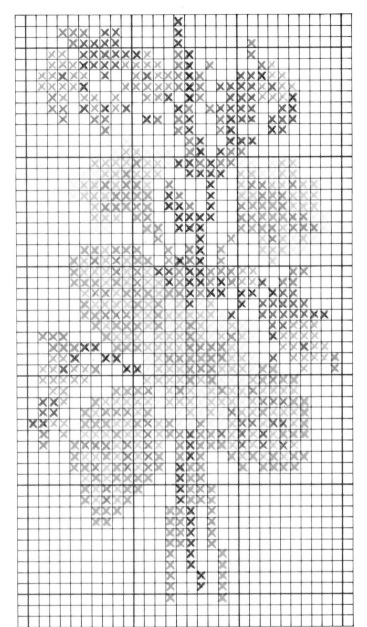

XXX	761	XXX	445	XXX	561
XXX	972	XXX	734	XXX	992
XXX	725	XXX	907	XXX	519
XXX	307	XXX	904	XXX	809

PRIMROSE AND FORGET-ME-NOT CUSHION

Previous page, the fresh yellows and blues of these spring flowers are always so welcome after the sombre colours of winter.

The cushion design is worked on white Hardanger fabric to give a very fresh feeling which echoes the clear, bright colours of the primrose and forget-me-not flowers when they first appear in the countryside.

MATERIALS
White Hardanger fabric (Zweigart E1008), 56cm (22in) square
Suitable backing fabric, 42cm (16½in) square
Cushion pad, 40cm (16in) square
DMC stranded embroidery threads:
  2 skeins each Green 472, 910; Blue 341, 800; 1 skein each Green 470, 704, 913; Brown 3064; Yellow 445, 743, 745, 972; Pink 761
DMC coton perlé No.5 thread: 1 skein Green 913
White sewing thread
Green sewing thread to match Green 913
Basting thread
Square wooden embroidery frame 50cm (20in)

TO MAKE THE CUSHION
1 Stretch the Hardanger fabric carefully on the frame, ensuring the straight grain is parallel to the sides of the frame.
2 Find the centre of the fabric by counting the threads. Mark with Basting Stitches the horizontal and vertical centre guidelines and so establish the centre of the fabric. This will also divide it into quarter sections.
3 Use three strands of embroidery thread at all times. Each Cross Stitch is worked over two horizontal and two vertical sets of threads of the fabric.
4 Carefully count along one of the guidelines from the centre to where the narrow green border pattern intersects the guidelines (see the chart on the right). Then, using the appropriate colour, work the narrow border pattern.

××× ×××	761
××× ×××	3064
××× ×××	972
××× ×××	743
××× ×××	445
××× ×××	745
××× ×××	472
××× ×××	704
××× ×××	470
××× ×××	910
××× ×××	913
××× ×××	800
××× ×××	341

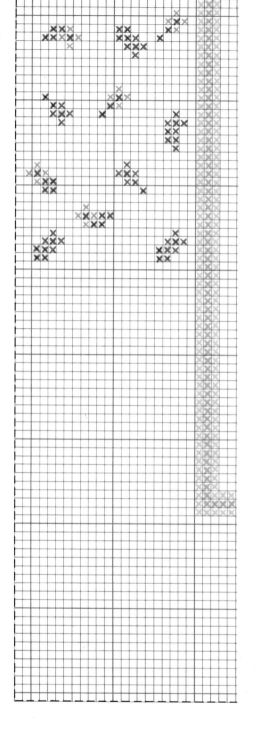

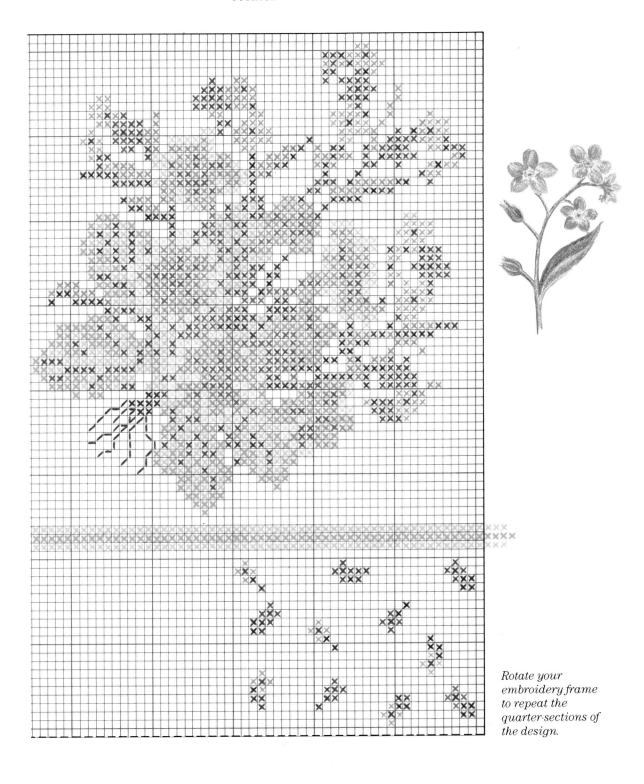

Rotate your
embroidery frame
to repeat the
quarter-sections of
the design.

67

5 Once this border has been worked, you will find it easy to position the four clumps of primroses and forget-me-nots within the quarter sections. Remember to make all the upper stitches of the Cross Stitches face the same direction in order to achieve an even effect.

6 Finally, work a line of Basting Stitches on the seam line to give the depth of the outer border. Then work a random pattern of tiny forget-me-not flowers and leaves around the outside of the green border. Try to place the tiny motifs to give a balanced effect even though they are worked randomly.

7 Remove the embroidery from the frame and trim away the surplus fabric, leaving a 1cm (⅜in) seam allowance on all sides.

Make up the cushion cover using the square of backing fabric, leaving an opening along one side to insert the cushion pad. Pin, baste and machine Straight Stitch the cushion face and backing fabric together. Carefully clip across the seam allowance at the corners and then turn the cushion cover to the right side. Press gently on the wrong side of the cushion.

8 Place the cushion pad inside the cover and close the opening with small Slip Stitches.

9 Make a twisted cord using the skein of green coton perlé thread. Divide the skein evenly into six lengths to make the cord (see Special Techniques page 133).

10 With matching sewing thread hand sew the cord evenly around the cushion. Tie a knot at each end of the cord and trim the excess yarn leaving a short length which can be teased to make mock tassels.

11 Sew the cords evenly along the sides of the cushion using the green sewing thread.

The motif of primroses and forget-me-nots could also be used on table linen. To make a stunning tablecloth work the motif four times around the centre point of the fabric and then work one motif in each corner, reversing the direction of the motif so that the plants point downwards.

The tiny stylized flowers that are scattered randomly around the border of the cushion echo the forget-me-nots of the centre motifs.

Wood Sorrel

*This dainty plant is a common woodland
find. Its gently curving stems, clover-like leaves and
white flowers with pink-tinged petals have
been the inspiration for this design which is shown on
the curtain tie-back and has been adapted
to be used with the basket.*

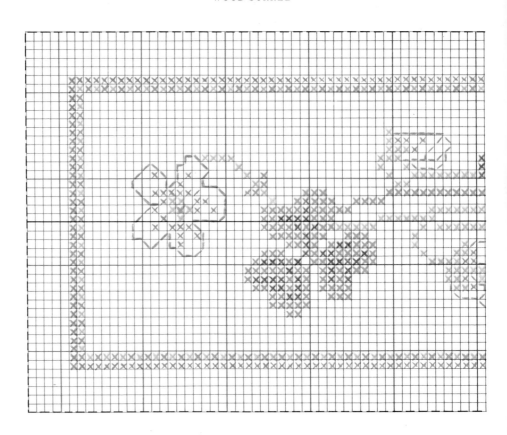

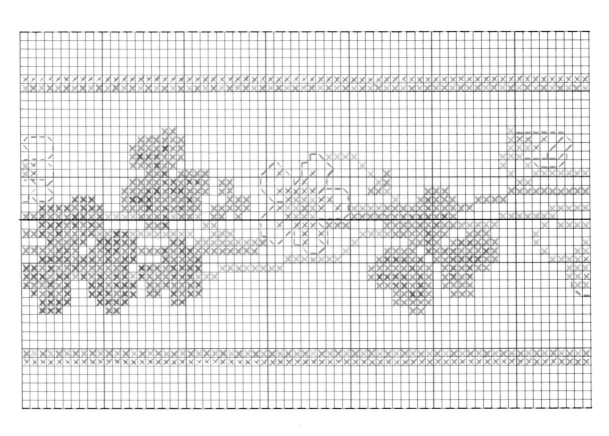

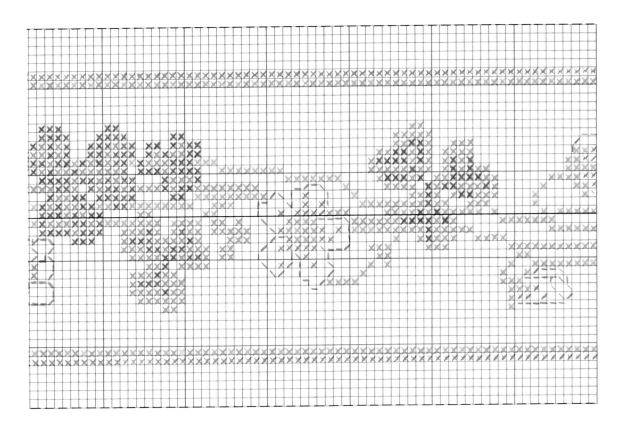

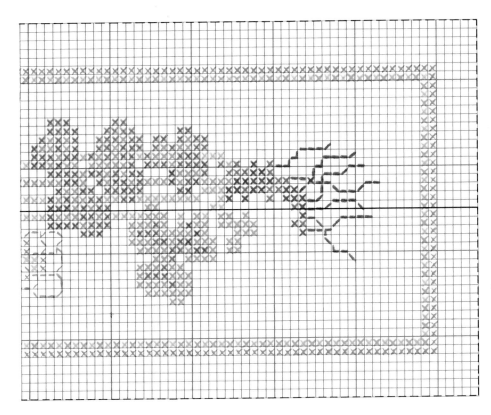

These charts give the entire design for the tie-back. Simply work the top chart from left to right then carry on the design by moving to the lower chart and you will find the design joins up.

WOOD SORREL
CURTAIN TIE-BACK

The wood sorrel plant has been used to give a linear design which is suitable for a curtain tie-back but would look equally attractive as a bell-pull. It would also be ideal worked in a strip to form a decorative border for table linen or bath linen with only a little adaptation.

MATERIALS
White Hardanger fabric (9 threads per cm, 22 per in), 15 × 60cm (6 × 24in)
White cotton backing fabric, 15 × 60cm (6 × 24in)
Fabric suitable for back of tie-back, 15 × 60cm (6 × 24in)
DMC stranded embroidery thread: 1 skein each Pink 3326; Green 470, 563, 472; small amounts of Brown 434, 437; Yellow 743
DMC coton perlé thread No.5: 1 skein each Green 563, 472
White and light green sewing thread
Basting thread
Small rotating embroidery frame

TO MAKE THE TIE-BACK
1 Mount the two short ends of the strip of Hardanger fabric on the rotating sides of the frame. Roll the excess fabric around one of these so that you are ready to start working the design at one end.
2 Count across the width of the fabric to find the centre holes and mark with a pin.
3 Use three strands of thread at all times except when working the roots, which should be embroidered using two strands of dark brown thread. Work each Cross Stitch over two horizontal and two vertical threads and remember to make all the upper stitches of the Cross Stitches face the same way. Begin the design at the top end of the chart on page 72 and work the border 3cm (1¼in) away from the fabric edge, accurately centring the design (as marked with the pin). Follow the chart downwards, adjusting the position of the fabric on the frame as necessary.

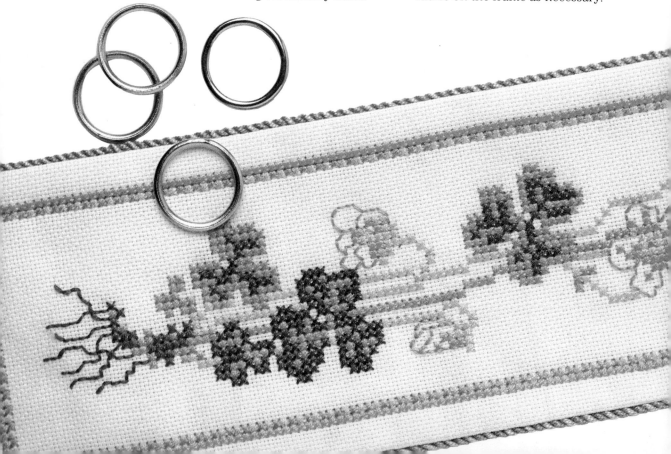

4 Once you have completed the Cross Stitch design remove the strip from the frame and gently press it on the wrong side. This will encourage the stitchery to stand out. Place this right side up over the white cotton backing fabric and baste the two layers together on the seam line (see the chart on pages 72–3 for position of the dotted seam line).

5 With right sides together, pin, baste and machine stitch the back and front of the tie-back together on the seam line. Leave the bottom edge open.

6 Trim away the excess fabric and clip carefully across the seam allowance at the corners. Gently press the tie-back on the wrong side and then turn it to the right side.

7 Turn in the seam allowance of the bottom opening and hand stitch the edges together, but do not finish off your thread.

8 Make a twisted cord approximately 140cm (55in) in length (see Special Techniques, page 133), using the two shades of Green coton perlé thread. Start at the bottom corner (where the open edges are waiting to be joined together) and ease open the seam at the last stitch to make a space so that you can tuck inside the beginning of the cord. Carefully stitch the cord all around the edge of the tie-back, then tuck in the end of the cord and finish off your thread securely to ensure the cord will not untwist.

9 Hand sew the curtain rings in position at the centre point of the back at the top and bottom of the tie-back, remembering that the stitches must not show on the front. If you are making a bell-pull rather than a curtain tie-back you will, of course, need only one ring which is positioned at the top edge.

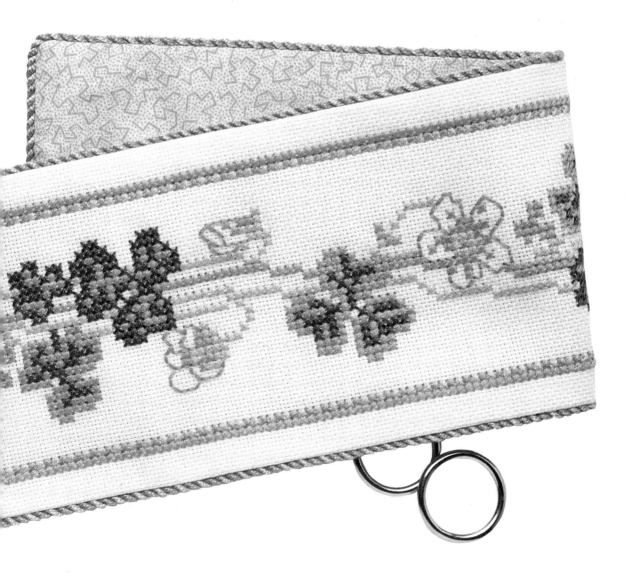

The delicate woodland plant is shown realistically in the centre of the basket lid and then stylized flower buds are scattered around the border.

WOOD SORREL BASKET WITH EMBROIDERED LID

This pretty, fabric-lined basket has a soft lid with lace edging and a simple, quickly worked design of wood sorrel in its centre circled by stylized flower buds. The basket could be used to hide away neatly all sorts of items such as cosmetics, toiletries, sewing notions or handkerchiefs.

The size of the basket used here measures 23cm (9in) diameter across its top and 17cm (7in) diameter across its base and has as depth of 9cm (3½in). The fabric requirements are given for this size. You can easily adapt the amount of fabric needed for a different sized basket, by making a paper pattern of the base and top diameters, and adding one and a half times the measurement around the sides of the basket for the gathered sides of the lining. (Always remember to allow for turnings when calculating the amounts of lining fabric required and, if you are using evenweave fabric, add an extra amount to enable you to place it within the embroidery hoop.)

MATERIALS

White Hardanger fabric (Zweigart E1008), 35cm (14in) square
Printed cotton fabric suitable for lining, 40 × 110cm (16 × 43in)
Pelmet weight interfacing (Vilene), 25 × 64cm (10 × 25in)
White gathered lace edging 2.5cm (1in) wide and 75cm (30in) long
DMC stranded embroidery thread: 1 skein each Pink 3326; Green 470, 472, 563; small amounts Brown 434, 437; Yellow 743
DMC coton perlé thread No.5: 1 skein each Green 472, 563
White sewing thread
Transparent nylon thread
Sewing thread to match either Green 472 or 563
Basting thread
Wooden embroidery hoop, 25cm (10in)

TO MAKE THE BASKET

1 Place the evenweave fabric centrally in the hoop, pulling the fabric carefully so that the working area is taut and the grain is straight.
2 Find, then mark with Basting Stitches, the horizontal and vertical guidelines. This will also give the centre of the working area.
3 Use three strands of embroidery thread at all times and work each Cross Stitch over two sets of horizontal and vertical threads making sure that all the upper stitches of the Cross Stitches face the same direction to give a smooth and even effect.
4 Following the chart on pages 80–1 work the wood sorrel design, beginning in the centre and working outwards, so that you have the central motif circled

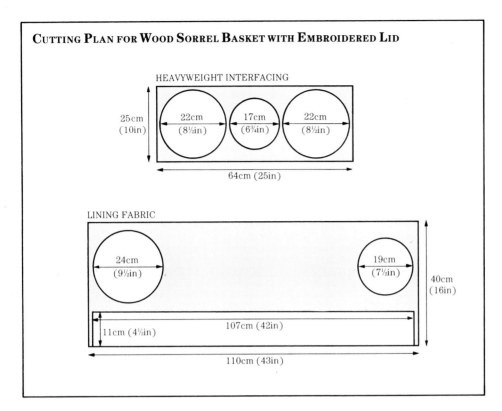

CUTTING PLAN FOR WOOD SORREL BASKET WITH EMBROIDERED LID

HEAVYWEIGHT INTERFACING

25cm (10in)

22cm (8½in)   17cm (6¾in)   22cm (8½in)

64cm (25in)

LINING FABRIC

24cm (9½in)   19cm (7½in)

40cm (16in)

11cm (4½in)   107cm (42in)

110cm (43in)

by two decorative bands. The roots of the central plant motif are worked in Back Stitch. Beyond the outer band the design is built up randomly, working lots of tiny stylized flowerbuds in order to achieve a scattered effect. Check the diameter of your basket lid at this stage and work the random pattern to a width that will reach just beyond the edge of the lid.

5 Once the stitchery is complete remove the evenweave fabric from the hoop and press it gently on the wrong side with a steam iron. This will encourage the stitchery to stand out with an embossed effect.

6 Keep a 1cm (⅜in) turning allowance but trim away the rest of the surplus fabric.

7 Following the cutting plan above, carefully and accurately cut out two circles from the interfacing, each measuring 22cm (8½in) in diameter. Then cut out a third, smaller circle measuring 17cm (6¾in) in diameter. (Keep the smaller circle to one side to be used for the basket base.)

8 Again following the cutting plan above, cut out a long strip of lining fabric measuring 11 × 107cm (4½ × 42in) and then two circles measuring 24cm (9½in) and 19cm (7½in) in diameter respectively. Keep the long strip and the smallest circle to one side to be used to line the basket.

9 Place the evenweave fabric circle over one of the large interfacing circles so that their centres line up and pin them together. Then, using basting thread, carefully fold the turning allowance over the edge of the interfacing and baste to hold. (Do not allow your stitches to show on the embroidered side as they remain permanently in place.) Similarly, place the larger lining circle over the remaining large interfacing circle and fold the turning allowance over the edge of the interfacing shape, basting to hold.

10 Using tiny Running or Back Stitches, attach the gathered lace edging around the underside of the edge of the evenweave lid and then neatly join the cut ends of the lace.

11 Place the lining lid circle under the evenweave circle and, with a double length of white sewing thread, join the layers together with small Slip Stitches.

434

437

3326

743

472

563

470

This is the chart for the lid of the basket. It could also be used to make a set of table mats. Drink mats could be made using only the central area of the design.

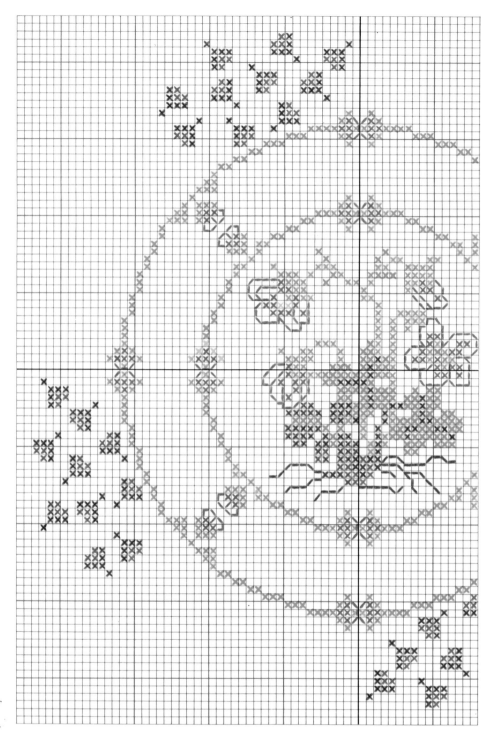

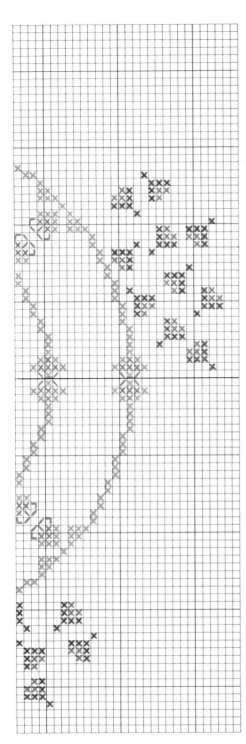

12 Make a two-colour twisted cord using the two shades of green coton perlé thread. Use four strands of each colour and make it approximately 90cm (36in) finished length (see Special Techniques on page 133). With green sewing thread attach the cord around the edge of the lid so that the ends overlap directly below the position of the roots of the central plant motif. Trim the cord ends neatly, knotting them and teasing out the loose threads to give mock tassels.

13 Line the basket in the following way. Cover the small interfacing circle with the circle of lining fabric in the same way as you covered the lid pieces (see Step 11). Join the short ends of the long strip together with a narrow seam. Along one raw edge of the continuous strip turn under 1cm (⅜in) to the wrong side. Then with a long, double length of white sewing thread, work a line of small, neat Gathering Stitches along the turned edge. This will gather the fabric and neaten it at the same time. Do not fasten off the gathering thread.

14 Work a line of Gathering Stitches along the other edge of the strip but do not turn and neaten it. Work a line of stitching 1cm (⅜in) in from the raw edge. Draw up this gathering thread so that the fabric fits around the base circle. With right sides together and working from the wrong side of the base, Slip Stitch the gathered fabric to the edge of the base.

15 Place the lining inside the basket and adjust to fit. Gather the upper edge of the lining to fit around the top of the basket, just below the rim, pinning the fabric into the basket as you go. Secure the gathering thread when you are satisfied that the lining fits the basket neatly and correctly. Then use transparent nylon thread to stitch the gathered edge carefully to the basket rim, passing your needle backwards and forwards through both the fabric and the woven pattern of the basket.

16 If you wish to attach the lid to the top of the basket, use the nylon thread to do this. You may prefer to leave it unattached so that it simply rests on the top of the basket rim.

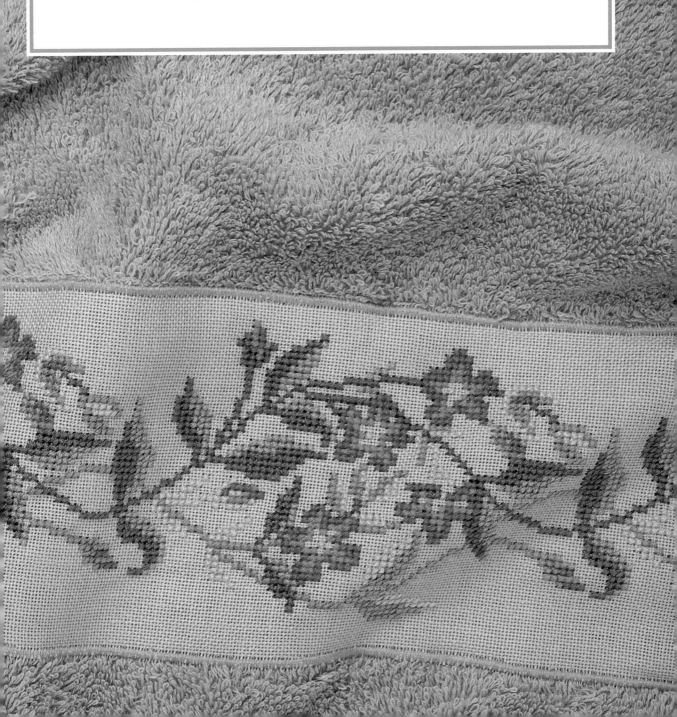

PERIWINKLE

*The periwinkle plant with its long,
trailing stems of beautifully shaped leaves and
starlike, purple flowers has been noted
since medieval times for its mystical as well as
medicinal properties. Today we can still
see it brightening up woodland, hedgerow and copse.*

XXX
XXX 904

XXX
XXX 471

XXX
XXX 992

XXX
XXX 955

XXX
XXX 3608

XXX
XXX 553

Repeat the charted area over and over again along your evenweave fabric to produce the towel border.

PERIWINKLE GUEST TOWEL

The repeat pattern used for the canvas-work cushion on page 89 has been used here to decorate the border of a guest towel. The pattern is simply worked in a long continuous strip of one set of entwined periwinkle stems, leaves and flowers trailing along the border.

MATERIALS

Pale green guest towel, approximately 40cm (16in) wide

Pale green evenweave fabric 'Linda' (Zweigart E1235 colour eau-de-Nil 760), 20 × 50cm (8 × 20in)

DMC stranded embroidery thread: 1 skein each Green 471, 904, 955, 992; Mauve 553, 3608

Green sewing thread to match towel

Small rotating embroidery frame

TO MAKE THE TOWEL BORDER

1 Stretch the strip of fabric on the rotating frame, rolling the excess length of the strip around one of the rotating sides of the frame.

2 Find the centre of the width of the fabric and using this as a guide simply work the border design along the length of the fabric. Each Cross Stitch is worked over two horizontal and two vertical threads of the fabric. Use three strands of thread at all times, which will give a small but full Cross Stitch on this quite fine gauge fabric. Remember to make all the upper stitches of the Cross Stitches face the same way to produce an even effect.

3 When you have worked a strip of the repeat pattern equal to the width of the guest towel (approximately 40cm [16in]), remove the fabric from the frame and press it gently on the wrong side with a steam iron. This will encourage the stitchery to stand out on the right side.

4 Trim away the excess fabric, leaving a 10cm (4in) wide strip that is the width of the towel plus 1cm (⅜in) at each end for a small turning.

5 Pin and baste the Cross Stitch border across one end of the towel, tucking in the narrow allowance at both ends. With green sewing thread, machine Satin Stitch along the raw edges of the border, covering them completely with the width of the Satin Stitching and attaching the strip to the towel securely.

6 Finally, Slip Stitch the turned allowances to the towel sides to complete this charming guest towel.

Overleaf, *the rich greens and purple complement each other in the entwined repeat pattern on the cushion and towel.*

PERIWINKLE CANVASWORK CUSHION

Cross Stitch has been used to work both the entwined design of the periwinkle and the background areas. If you wish, you could work the background in a smaller Half Cross Stitch (Tent Stitch) to create a contrasting effect. Similarly, if worked on an evenweave fabric you do not have to 'fill in' the background, and this will create another effect.

MATERIALS

White mono canvas (15 holes per in), 56cm (22in) square
DMC Tapisserie wool: 14 skeins Ecru; 5 skeins each Green 7542, 7385; 4 skeins Green 7369; 3 skeins each Green 7382, Purple 7895; 2 skeins Magenta 7153
Green fabric suitable to back cushion, 40cm (16in) square
Cushion pad, 38cm (15in) square
Sewing thread to match Green 7542
Wooden frame, 50cm (20in) square
Waterproof marking pen

TO MAKE THE CUSHION

1 Stretch the canvas on the frame, ensuring the threads are parallel to the sides of the frame.

2 Using the waterproof marking pen, measure and then mark on the canvas, a 38cm (15in) square. Then within this square carefully measure and mark out the grid pattern of the all-over repeat design. Each square of the chart represents one Cross Stitch, which in turn is worked over two horizontal and two vertical threads of canvas. The repeat pattern for this design fits together in the same way as a brick wall pattern. (See page 90 for how the pattern repeats.) Start at one side of your square on the canvas and work across, drawing in the vertical lines. Then add the staggered horizontal lines. This grid pattern will help you when working the Cross Stitches upon the canvas as you will have guidelines to ensure you are following the design accurately.

3 Follow the chart using the colour key for Tapisserie wools and remember to work your Cross Stitches so that all the upper parts of the stitches face the same direction to produce an even effect. Do not use very long lengths of yarn as the action of passing the soft woollen yarn backwards and forwards through the holes of the canvas will wear it thin. You will find it easier if you start with the darker green sections of the stems and leaves as they give a good framework upon which to build your design. Then you can easily locate the other areas.

4 Once you have completed the entwined design fill in the background, being as economical as possible with your yarn.

5 Remove the completed cushion face from the frame and trim the excess canvas, leaving a 1cm (⅜in) seam allowance on all sides. With right sides facing, pin then baste and machine Straight Stitch the cushion face and back together along the edge of the canvaswork stitchery. Remember to leave an opening along one side to push the cushion pad in. Carefully clip across the seam allowance at the corners. Turn to the right side and fill with the cushion pad. Fold in the seam allowance along the opening and Slip Stitch the folded edges together to close.

6 Make four equal lengths of twisted cord as follows, using the two complete skeins of Green 7542 yarn. Carefully unravel each skein and cut in half. Then divide each half once more into three equal lengths and use to make a cord. Repeat with the other groups of yarn to make three more cords (see Special Techniques page 133).

7 Carefully hand stitch one cord along each side of the cushion. Tie a knot in each cord at the corners and trim the excess yarn leaving a short length which can be teased to make a mock tassel.

8 Sew the cords evenly along the sides of the cushion using the green thread.

Opposite, *the close-up view of the cushion shows the soft woollen texture of the yarns used.*

XXX
XXX   7385

XXX
XXX   7382

XXX
XXX   7542

XXX
XXX   7369

XXX
XXX   7153

XXX
XXX   7895

▦   Ecru

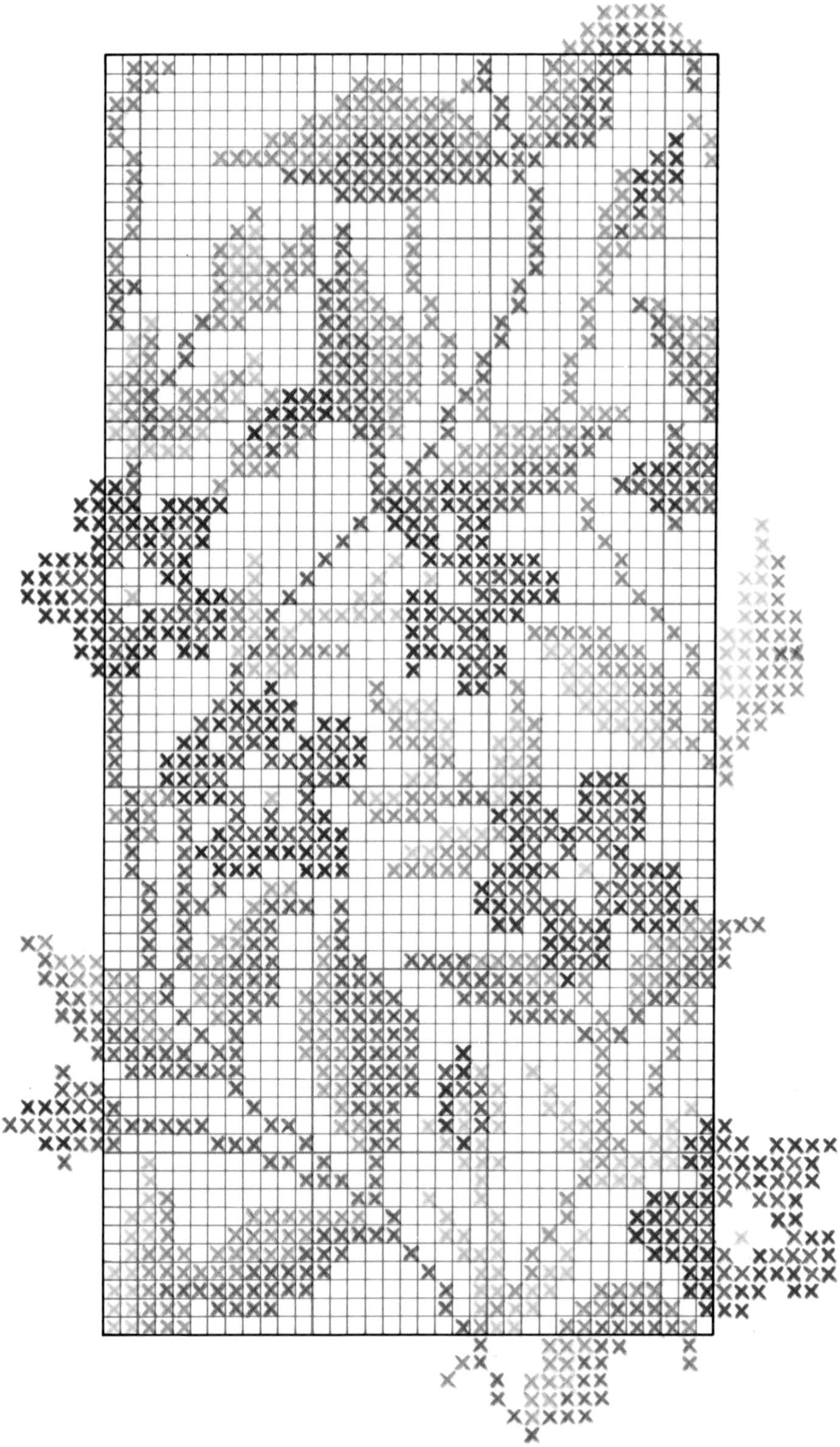

*The border
pattern of the
guest towel has
been arranged so
that it becomes an
all-over repeat
design.*

*Each complete
brick of the wall
pattern is 35
Cross Stitches
across by 70
down. Draw in the
vertical lines first
on your canvas.
Then add the
horizontal lines.*

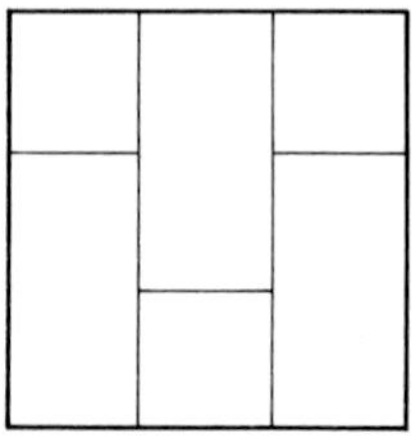

WILD STRAWBERRY

*This delightful creeping plant is often
found on dry grassland and in woodland. It has
small, white, starry flowers from April to
July followed by bright red fruits which often have a
much stronger flavour than their
cultivated garden cousins.*

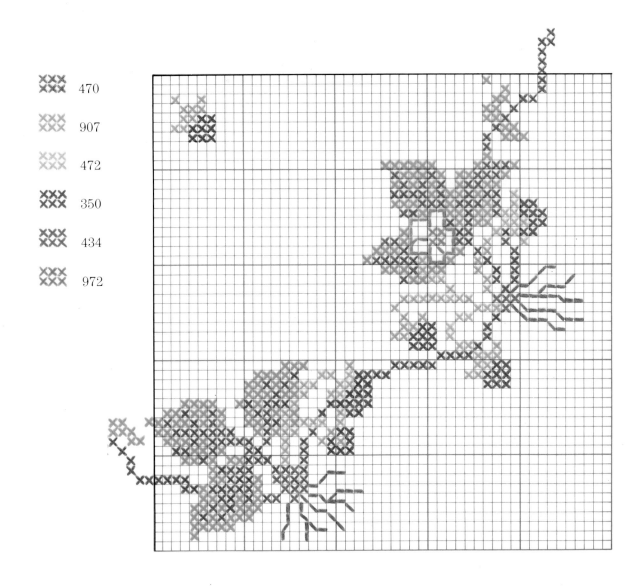

470

907

472

350

434

972

When this quarter-section of the border design is repeated around the jam pot cover it gives a continuous pattern of tiny strawberry plants. The single strawberry fruit is also used to decorate the plain corners of the table napkins.

WILD STRAWBERRY JAM POT COVERS

A pot of home-made strawberry jam or jelly with one of these pretty covers will make a very special gift and brighten up the tea tray or table.

They are quick and easy to make and could also be used as table mats as they are simply circular pieces of fabric with the design worked in the centre or around the edges, finished with a decorative narrow lace trimming to neaten the cut edge.

MATERIALS

(For two jam pot covers with centre designs and one with the border design)
2 circles white Hardanger fabric (Zweigart E1008), 23cm (9in) in diameter
1 circle white Fine Aida fabric (Zweigart E3706), 25cm (10in) in diameter
DMC stranded embroidery thread:
   1 skein each Green 470, 472, 907; Red 350; Yellow 972; Brown 434
White cotton lace edging, 6mm (¼in) wide and 2m (2¼yd) long
Satin ribbon to match Green 470, 3mm (⅛in) wide and 2m (2¼yd) long
White sewing thread
Pale coloured pencil
Wooden embroidery hoop 20cm (8in) in diameter

TO MAKE THE JAM POT COVERS

1 Choose which motif you wish to work. The border design is worked on the Fine Aida fabric and the two central designs are both worked on the Hardanger fabric.

2 *For the designs with a central motif* place the evenweave fabric centrally within the hoop. Mark with Basting Stitches the centre horizontal and vertical guidelines which will mark the centre of the circle and divide the working area into quarter segments. When working the central design of the straw-berry plant with ripe red fruits use the top motif of the repeat design following the chart on page 100. Use the solid black lines as your centre guidelines to help you position the design in the middle of the fabric. Omit the dark green Cross Stitches which represent the runners above the top fruit and also those from the root area. Work each Cross Stitch over two horizontal and two vertical sets of threads and similarly work the Back Stitches of the roots over two sets of threads. Remember to make all the upper stitches of the Cross Stitches face the same direction in order to produce an even effect.

The small white flowers of the strawberry plant (which forms the second design with a central motif) are worked in Back Stitch. These Back Stitches give the outline of each petal and there are also four Cross Stitches to represent each flower centre. Work these Back Stitches in the same way as those of the roots. When you have finished working the design go on to step 4.

✗✗✗ ✗✗✗	470
✗✗✗ ✗✗✗	907
✗✗✗ ✗✗✗	472
✗✗✗ ✗✗✗	434
✗✗✗ ✗✗✗	972

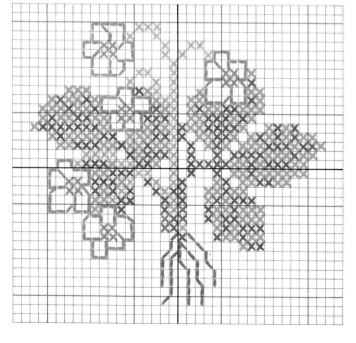

The jam pot covers can also be used as place mats.

3 *The border design* is worked on the Fine Aida fabric which shows the stitch size very clearly. Place the fabric in a hoop and, once more, find and mark with Basting Stitches the centre horizontal and vertical guidelines. Use these lines to help you position and work the four centre strawberries and then the circular border of strawberry plants. Use Back Stitches to represent the roots and the edges of the tiny white petals.

4 When you have completed the stitchery of your jam pot covers, remove the fabric from the hoop and press the fabric gently on the wrong side with a steam iron. This will encourage the stitchery to stand out with an embossed effect.

5 Turn the embroidered fabric over to the wrong side and, using the lines of Basting Stitches to give you the centre point, lightly draw with a pale-coloured pencil a circle 18cm (7¼in) in diameter for the central motifs and 20cm (8in) diameter for the border design. Cut around the drawn lines with a pair of sharp-pointed trimming scissors and remove the excess fabric.

6 Baste the narrow lace trimming around the raw edge of the fabric and with white sewing thread and a Zigzag Stitch machine the lace to the fabric to neaten the edge and prevent it from fraying. Hand stitch the cut ends of the lace edging together to neaten the finished cover.

7 The jam pot cover is held in place over the jam pot with the use of an elastic band and a length of the narrow satin ribbon, tied into a neat bow. However, if you wish, you can work a line of Zigzag Stitch around the centre area of the cover and thread the ribbon through this, but you will need to place the cover over the jam pot to measure the size of the circle before stitching.

The wild strawberry designs shown can be used in many ways to create items for use in your home. You could work a single motif on to a drinks mat, or adapt a circular jam-pot cover design to make a pretty round tray cloth. By varying the colours of the background material you can create different effects with a linked theme.

Overleaf, *the decorated jam pot lids nestle among the leaves of strawberry plants.*

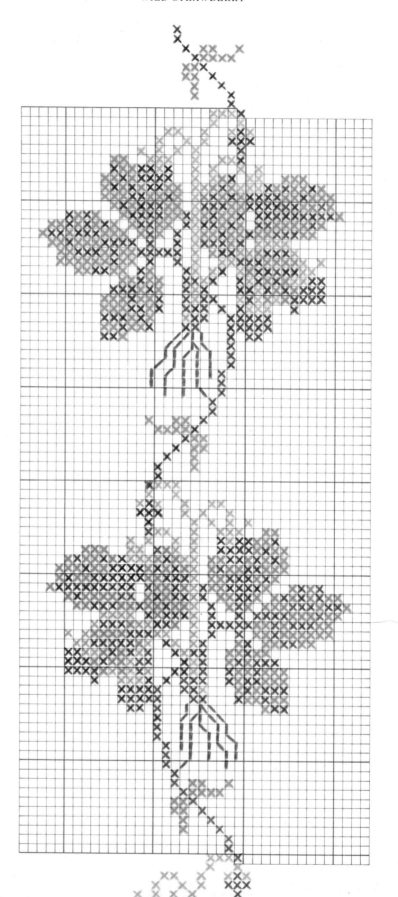

987

907

913

350

434

*Work the two
strawberry plants
and their runners
along each
napkin strip.
Only work the top
plant on each
napkin, so that
the dotted line
corresponds with
the basting
stitches on the
napkin square.*

WILD STRAWBERRY
NAPKINS AND NAPKIN RINGS

With thoughts of leisurely summer teas taken in the garden, these pretty napkins and matching rings have been inspired by the wild strawberry plant. The design has been simply constructed: a single motif of a plant with its tiny fruits has been drawn and then its mirror image has been positioned centrally below it and linked with a twisting runner. This repeat design could easily and effectively be used to decorate a border on towels, table linens, along the hem of a curtain and on a matching tie-back. Here it has been used to decorate the napkin rings by using just two linked motifs and then a single motif has been worked in one corner of each napkin.

MATERIALS
(For two napkins and matching rings)
'Linda' fabric (Zweigart E1235 colour
    760 eau-de-Nil), 90 × 85cm
    (36 × 33in)
DMC stranded embroidery thread:
    1 skein each Green 907, 913, 987;
    Red 350; Brown 434
Green sewing thread to match fabric
    or Green 913
2 small buttons
Wooden embroidery hoop, 18cm (7in)
    in diameter
Wooden embroidery hoop, 10cm (4in)
    in diameter
Pale green coloured pencil

This design can be worked as a continuous border pattern simply by repeating the plants and runners over and over again.

TO MAKE EACH NAPKIN

1 Carefully measure and then cut out two squares each measuring 45cm (18in) for the two napkins. Then from the remaining fabric cut out four strips each measuring 15 × 25cm (6 × 10in) for the napkin rings and linings.

2 Put the strips to one side. Press the two squares of fabric and with a pale green coloured pencil, lightly mark a 38cm (15in) square centrally within the fabric, making sure the sides of the square lie along the threads of the evenweave fabric.

3 Set your sewing machine to a decorative edging stitch (you may wish to work several trials on the spare fabric and choose which is the most effective) and with green sewing thread work along the marked lines around the square to give the edge of your first napkin. Securely fasten the threads. Do not cut away the excess fabric at this stage.

4 Use three strands of embroidery thread at all times and work each Cross Stitch over two horizontal and two vertical threads of fabric, following the chart on page 100. Remember to make all the upper stitches of the Cross Stitches face the same way to produce an even effect. The roots of the plants are worked in Back Stitch, each stitch being made over two threads of fabric. At one corner of your napkin count ten Cross Stitches in from the machined edge along the two converging sides and then baste to mark this line at the corner. This will allow you to place your strawberry motif (see top plant of repeat design) correctly in the corner. Place this corner within the larger embroidery hoop and work the strawberry plant motif omitting the darker green Cross Stitches which represent the twisting runner above the top fruit and the runner leading from the root area.

5 Once this motif is complete reposition the hoop so that you can work a small strawberry motif (see the chart on page 94) in each of the other three corners. Once more count ten Cross Stitches in from the machined edge of the napkin to find your starting point. Then place each fruit so that it points out towards the corner.

6 Press the napkin carefully on the wrong side with a steam iron and with sharp-pointed trimming scissors cut away the excess fabric close to the outer edge of the decorative machine stitching to complete the napkin.

TO MAKE EACH NAPKIN RING

1 Count the threads across the width of one of the strips of evenweave fabric to find the centre and then mark with Basting Stitches this centre line down the length of the strip. Begin the stitchery 5cm (2in) in from the short end and follow the chart on page 100, working your Cross Stitches as for the napkins, with the fabric stretched within the smaller embroidery hoop. You will only need to work two strawberry plant motifs, joined by the runner, for each napkin ring.

2 Once you have completed the stitchery remove the fabric from the hoop and press it carefully on the wrong side with a steam iron.

3 Place the embroidered strip face up over one of the remaining pieces of fabric and baste them together.

4 Using the green sewing thread and the same decorative machine stitch as used for the napkins, work a rectangle around the motifs to give the finished size of 7.5 × 17cm (3 × 6¾in). Securely fasten the ends of the thread and then with sharp-pointed trimming scissors remove the excess fabric outside the stitching to form the napkin ring.

5 Work a neat, hand-stitched button loop, using green sewing thread, centrally along the edge of the upper short end. Then securely sew a button in the middle of the other end of the strip, approximately 1cm (⅜in) in from the edge to complete the napkin ring. The ring is then formed by passing a button through the button loop.

These designs lend themselves to adaptations for other items. The pattern of the napkin ring can be repeated as often as necessary to form a decorative border on a guest towel or other bath linen. The single large motif used on the napkin would make a delightful gift card (see pages 41 and 110 for instructions on how to make the card).

Opposite, cream teas in the summer are enhanced with these delightful napkins and matching napkin rings.

WILD CYCLAMEN

*Although much admired and tenderly
cultivated in gardens, these small plants are now
rarely seen in the wild except perhaps in
sheltered, wooded areas. Unusually, the leaves do not
appear until the dainty flowers have died
in late autumn.*

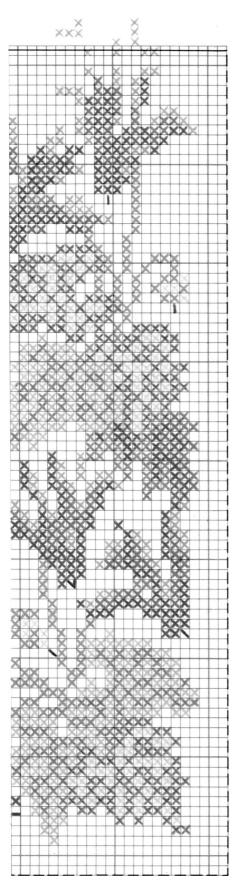

WILD CYCLAMEN CUSHION

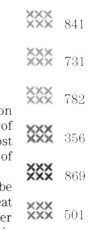

✕✕✕	315
✕✕✕	841
✕✕✕	731
✕✕✕	782
✕✕✕	356
✕✕✕	869
✕✕✕	501
✕✕✕	469
✕✕✕	503
✕✕✕	368
✕✕✕	223
✕✕✕	917
✕✕✕	3608
✕✕✕	605

This stunning cushion is worked on Pearl Aida fabric with dense areas of richly worked stitchery which almost entirely hide the cream background of the fabric.

Although the design appears to be complex, it is worked as four repeat quarter sections and is therefore easier to work than you may have thought. It is built up of small, wild cyclamen motifs which have been designed to fit together in a simple pattern, plus a richly coloured band of autumnal oak leaves which complement the colours of the cyclamen flowers so well.

MATERIALS
Cream Pearl Aida fabric (Zweigart
    E1007 colour 264; 11 stitches per
    inch), 56cm (22in) square
DMC stranded embroidery thread:
    3 skeins Brown 841; Green 368;
    2 skeins Brown 315, 782; Green 501,
    503, 731; Mauve 917, 1 skein Brown
    356, 869; Green 469; Mauve 605,
    3608; Pink 223
DMC coton perlé No.5 thread: 1 skein
    Mauve 718
Suitable fabric for back of cushion,
    40cm (16in) square
Cream sewing thread
Sewing thread to match Mauve 718
Cushion pad, 38cm (15in) square
Basting thread
Wooden frame, 50cm (20in) square

TO MAKE THE CUSHION
1 Stretch the Pearl Aida fabric carefully on the frame, ensuring the straight grain is parallel to the sides of the frame.
2 Find the centre of the fabric by counting the sets of threads. Mark with Basting Stitches the horizontal and vertical guidelines and so establish the centre of the fabric. This will also divide it into quarter sections.

NB: With this design the guidelines run through a set of threads, giving a central Cross Stitch rather than a central hole.
3 Use three strands of thread at all times. Each Cross Stitch is worked over one horizontal and one vertical set of threads which are clearly defined in this type of the fabric.
4 Working from the chart on pages 106–7, carefully count along one of the guidelines to locate where you wish to commence stitching. You may choose to start in the centre, working the golden brown oak leaves, or you may prefer to count outwards to the inner green border and work around this first. Wherever you commence, double check that you have counted the correct number of Cross-Stitch spaces.
5 To conserve materials, fasten your thread securely after finishing a section and then begin again elsewhere, rather than jumping across the wrong side of the fabric. Remember to form all the Cross Stitches so that the upper stitches are all facing the same direction in order to achieve an even effect.
6 Continue working and methodically build up the design, repeating each quarter section accurately. It will help if you turn your embroidery frame around, once you have completed the first quarter, so that the next quarter section will be facing you ready to be worked.
7 Once the design is complete use the chart to locate the seam line of the cushion and mark this with Basting Stitches around the embroidery.
8 Remove the embroidered fabric from the frame and trim away the surplus fabric, leaving a 1cm (⅜in) seam allowance on all sides.
9 Make the cushion cover using the square of backing fabric, leaving an opening along one side to insert the cushion pad. Pin the right side of the embroidery to the right side of the backing fabric and tack along the line of basting. Machine Straight Stitch around the line of basting, trim the seam allowance across the corners and turn the cushion to the right side. If necessary, press the cover gently on the wrong side to encourage the stitchery to stand out with an embossed effect.
10 Place the cushion pad inside the cover and close the opening with small Slip Stitches.
11 Make a long twisted cord using the skein of coton perlé thread by dividing it evenly into six lengths (see Special Techniques, page 133).
12 With matching sewing thread, hand stitch the cord around the cushion, knot the ends of the cord and tease out any surplus cord to make mock tassels.

The rich autumnal colours of oak leaves are used to enrich this design and complement the purple flowers of cyclamen plants.

WILD CYCLAMEN GIFT CARD

Handmade gift cards are always greatly appreciated as they have been personally made by the sender. However, they do not take long to work and can also be mounted within a small frame to make a permanent wall picture.

This gift card can be quickly and easily made by working just one of the side motifs of the outer border of the wild cyclamen cushion design on pages 106-7. If you wish, you can extract other parts of the cushion chart and use these to work different motifs for gift cards of different sizes and shapes.

MATERIALS

Purchased gift card, dark green, 11 × 15.75cm (4½ × 6¼in) with a rectangular window measuring 7 × 11cm (2¾ × 4½in)

Cream Pearl Aida fabric (Zweigart E1007 colour 264), 20cm (8in) square

Small amounts of DMC stranded embroidery thread: Green 368, 469, 501, 503; Brown 315, 356, 841; Pink 223; Mauve 605, 917, 3608

Clear adhesive glue suitable for fabric and card

Wooden embroidery hoop, 15cm (6in) diameter

TO MAKE THE GIFT CARD

1 Place the fabric in the hoop, making sure the grain of the fabric is straight.

2 Following the cushion chart on pages 106-7 work one of the side plant motifs in the centre of your fabric. Use three strands of thread at all times. Each Cross Stitch is worked over one horizontal and one vertical set of threads.

3 Once the plant motif is complete remove the fabric from the hoop. Press the wrong side of fabric gently with a steam iron, to give the stitchery an embossed effect.

4 Open the card out flat and place the window section of it over the cyclamen motif. Estimate how much fabric has to be cut away then trim the surplus so that the design fits within the frame but allows a border to overlap and be glued to the card.

5 Use the clear glue to hold the design centrally within the window and then fold the backing section over the wrong side of the design and glue them together to complete the gift card.

By changing the colour of the mounting card and backing fabric, you can alter the appearance of the gift card.

WILD CYCLAMEN
SCENTED SACHET

This pretty scented sachet can be worked quickly to make a delightful gift, using only small amounts of fabric and thread. The design of the cyclamen plants which are worked in each corner is the same as that worked in the corners of the cushion. A very simple and stylized motif is used to decorate the centre of the sachet and this is linked to the outer motifs with bands of mauve and green Cross Stitches.

With a little adaptation the sachet motifs, together with those of the cushion, can be used to decorate other items such as a square box using the sachet design for the lid and a gift card motif on each of the four sides.

MATERIALS

Cream Pearl Aida fabric (Zweigart E1007 colour 264), 30cm (12in) square
Cream cotton fabric for back of cushion, 23cm (9in) square
2 pieces of cream cotton lining fabric, 23cm (9in) square
DMC stranded embroidery thread:
    1 skein each Green 368, 469, 501, 503; Pink 223; Mauve 605, 917, 3608; Brown 869
Cream sewing thread
Cream cotton gathered lace edging, 2cm (¾in) wide, 90cm (36in) long
Small amount of Kapok or other filling
Pot pourri or other scented herb
Wooden frame, 25cm (10in) square

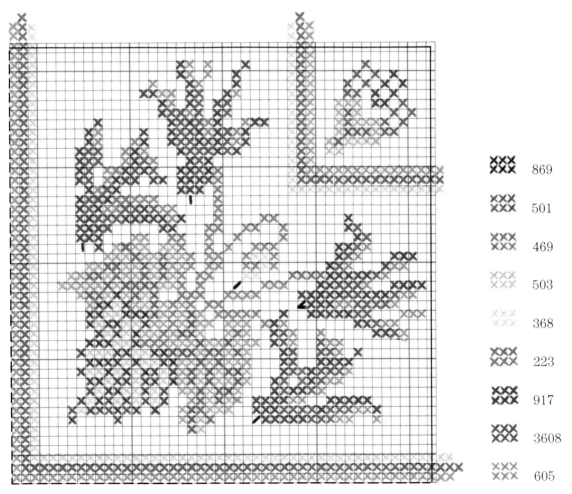

✗✗✗	869
✗✗✗	501
✗✗✗	469
✗✗✗	503
✗✗✗	368
✗✗✗	223
✗✗✗	917
✗✗✗	3608
✗✗✗	605

To Make the Scented Sachet

1 Stretch the Pearl Aida fabric carefully on the frame, ensuring the straight grain is parallel to the sides of the frame.
2 Find the centre of the fabric by counting the sets of threads. Mark with Basting Stitches the horizontal and vertical centre guidelines and so establish the centre of the fabric. This will also divide it into quarter sections.
NB As with the wild cyclamen cushion the guidelines run through a set of threads giving a central Cross Stitch rather than a central hole.
3 Use three strands of thread at all times. Each Cross Stitch is worked over one horizontal and one vertical set of threads.
4 Carefully count along one of the guidelines to locate the position of the inner band of Cross Stitches and work this following the chart on page 111. Then work the centre motifs.
5 Count outwards from the inner band and work the outer three-coloured band, then work each of the four corner motifs of cyclamen plants. These corner motifs are the same as those used on the cushion.
6 Once the stitchery is complete remove the fabric from the frame and trim the surplus fabric leaving a 1cm (⅜in) seam allowance all around the outer edge of the stitchery.
7 Pin and baste the gathered lace edging to the right side of the sachet face on the seam line (outer edge of stitchery). Over this place the sachet backing fabric (right side facing right side) and machine Straight Stitch around the sachet on the seam line, leaving a small opening on one side.
8 Turn the sachet to the right side and neatly join the cut ends of the lace edging together with cream sewing thread.
9 Make the lining bag using the two squares of cotton fabric to produce a finished size of 19cm (7½in) square. Leave a small opening. Turn the bag to the right side and fill with the kapok and pot pourri. Tuck in the edges of the opening and hand Slip Stitch the folded edges together.
10 Place the lining bag inside the sachet and close the opening with neat Slip Stitches.
11 Finally, make four mock tassels.
To make a tassel cut six 2.5cm (1in) lengths of Mauve 3608 DMC stranded embroidery thread and place them together in a neat bundle at one corner of the sachet. Thread a length of matching yarn in a needle and tightly stitch over and around the middle of the bundle of cut lengths several times, catching the corner point of the fabric in order to attach them securely to the sachet. Gently tease out the individual strands of the thread to make them look like a tassel.

To finish off, make three more mock tassels, one for each of the other corners of the sachet.

The gracefully shaped corner motifs of the cushion appear much more dominant when they are worked on the smaller scented sachet.

KINGCUP

The kingcup, also known as marsh marigold, can be found from early spring until late summer in damp and shady areas such as windswept marshes and wet woodlands. It brightens up its surroundings with strong yellow flowers and equally splendid glossy leaves.

KINGCUP MIRROR FRAME

The design is used to create a rectangular border of kingcups growing strongly upwards and around the frame of a mirror. The crisp white Hardanger fabric emphasizes the freshness of the design and its colours.

The frame could also be used to display a favourite photograph, or you could work the design and then make it into a cushion.

MATERIALS
White Hardanger fabric (Zweigart E1008), 40 × 50cm (16 × 20in)
Cotton fabric of suitable print for back of frame, 30 × 37cm (12 × 14½in)
2 rectangles of heavyweight (pelmet) interfacing, each 28 × 35cm (11 × 14in)
Rectangle of firm white cardboard, 28 × 35cm (11 ×14in)
DMC stranded embroidery thread: 1 skein each Green 469, 472, 502, 734, 890, 907, 3347; Yellow 445, 726, 742, 973
DMC coton perlé No.5 thread: 1 skein Green 3347
White sewing thread
Green sewing thread to match Green 3347
Two small curtain rings
Mirror, minimum size 15 × 23cm (6 × 9in), maximum size 27 × 34cm (10¾ × 13½in)
Strong adhesive glue suitable for glass and cardboard
Sharp craft knife
Rectangular embroidery frame

TO MAKE THE MIRROR FRAME
1 Mount the Hardanger fabric on the frame, ensuring that the threads of the fabric are parallel to the sides of the frame.
2 Find and mark with Basting Stitches the horizontal and vertical centre guide-

lines to establish the centre of the working area.

3 Carefully count outwards from the centre, along one of the basting lines to commence stitching. Use three strands of embroidery thread at all times.

Each Cross Stitch is worked over two horizontal and two vertical sets of threads. Remember to make all the upper stitches of the Cross Stitches face the same direction in order to achieve an even effect. Do not jump across the wrong side of the fabric from one area to another of the same colour. Always fasten off the thread and start again as the thread may show through to the right side as well as being untidy and uneconomical. Work around the frame carefully, following the charts overleaf.

4 Once you have completed the design remove the fabric from the frame and press it gently on the wrong side with a steam iron to encourage an embossed effect. *Do not remove the basting threads.*

5 Using your embroidered design and the chart to guide you, centrally measure, mark and then carefully cut out a window from one piece of heavyweight interfacing and from the piece of cardboard. Lightly mark the half-way points along the sides and the top and bottom of the interfacing 'window'. With the right side facing downwards place the embroidered fabric on a clean, flat surface. Place the interfacing window over it, aligning the half-way marks of the window with the basting threads of the embroidered fabric.

6 Pin and baste the layers together and then carefully cut out the centre section of the embroidered fabric, allowing a 1cm (⅜in) turning on all sides. Clip the fabric in towards the corners of the interfacing frame.

7 Turn the fabric allowance over the edge of the window and baste to hold, paying particular attention to the corners. Do not baste through to the right side of the embroidery as these stitches will remain permanently in place.

8 Trim away the excess fabric around the outside edges of the interfacing frame allowing a 1cm (⅜in) turning.

Fold this to the wrong side of the frame and baste to hold in place, remembering not to stitch through to the right side of the frame.

9 With the right side facing downwards, place the print fabric on a clean flat surface and put the remaining piece of interfacing centrally on top of it. Turn and baste the allowance to the wrong side of the interfacing, again remembering not to stitch through all the layers to the right side of the back of the mirror frame.

10 Set your sewing machine to a decorative stitch of your choice and with green sewing thread work a border around the edge of the back of the mirror frame, approximately 6mm (¼in) from the edge. This edging not only decorates the back of the frame but also firmly attaches the fabric to the interfacing.

11 Hand stitch two curtain rings to the back, approximately 8cm (3¼in) down from the top edge and 4cm (1½in) in from the sides.

12 Using a double length of white sewing thread, Slip Stitch the back and front of the frame together leaving the top edge open.

13 Glue the mirror in position behind the cardboard window frame and allow the adhesive to set thoroughly. (If in doubt about the strength of the glue you can use masking tape as well.)

14 Trim away a *very small* amount from each edge of the cardboard frame to allow it to be carefully passed into the frame. Once in position Slip Stitch the top edges of the frame together to complete the mirror frame.

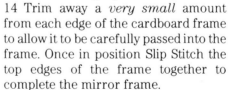

✗✗✗ ✗✗✗	890
✗✗✗ ✗✗✗	469
✗✗✗ ✗✗✗	502
✗✗✗ ✗✗✗	3347
✗✗✗ ✗✗✗	907
✗✗✗ ✗✗✗	472
✗✗✗ ✗✗✗	734
✗✗✗ ✗✗✗	742
✗✗✗ ✗✗✗	973
✗✗✗ ✗✗✗	726
✗✗✗ ✗✗✗	445

Overleaf, *the kingcups around the towel and mirror frame evoke a watery mood.*

✗✗✗ ✗✗✗	890
✗✗✗ ✗✗✗	469
✗✗✗ ✗✗✗	502
✗✗✗ ✗✗✗	3347
✗✗✗ ✗✗✗	907
✗✗✗ ✗✗✗	472
✗✗✗ ✗✗✗	734
✗✗✗ ✗✗✗	742
✗✗✗ ✗✗✗	973
✗✗✗ ✗✗✗	726
✗✗✗ ✗✗✗	445

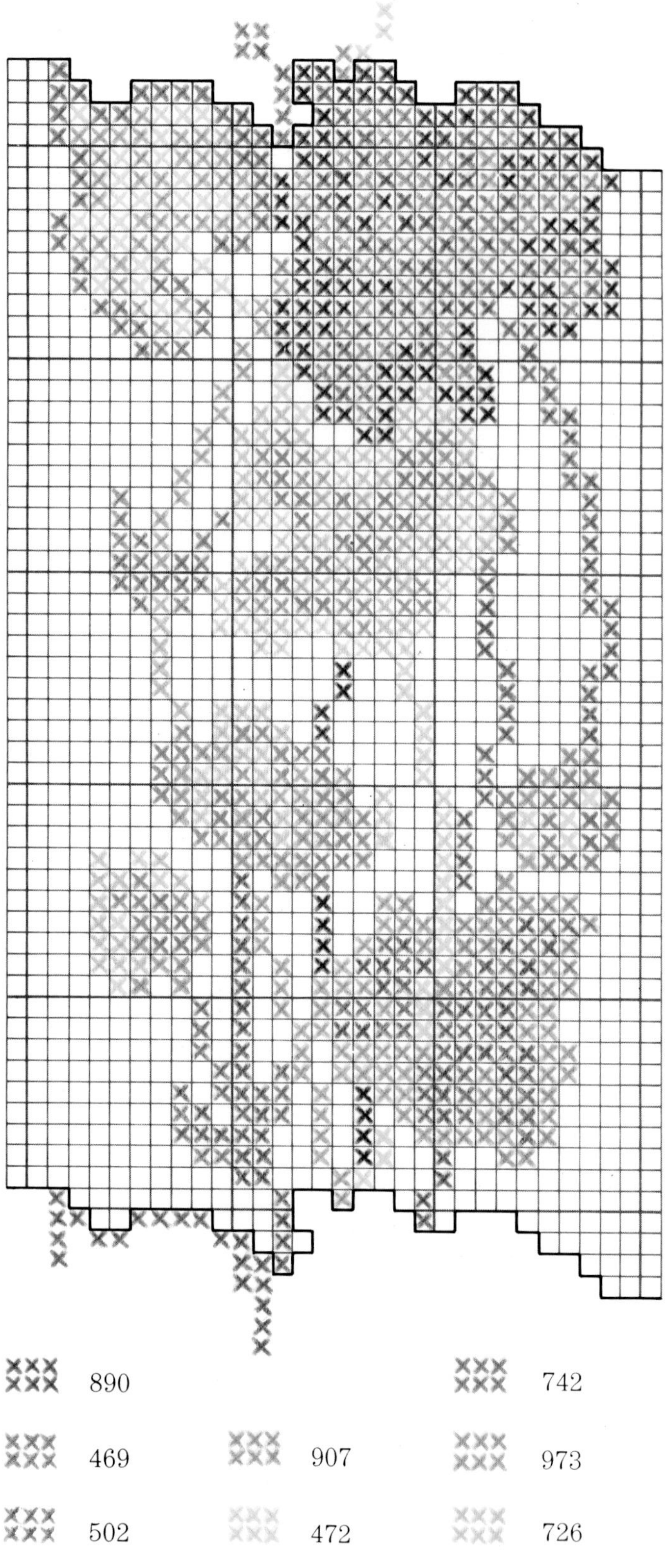

KINGCUP HAND TOWEL

The clear yellows and greens of the kingcup will cheer your bathroom when used to decorate the towels. The border pattern, which repeats to form a striking design, has been taken from the central section of the side of the mirror frame design (see page 116).

MATERIALS

Pale yellow hand towel, approximately 58cm (23in) wide

White Hardanger fabric (Zweigart E1008), 15 × 70cm (6 × 28in)

DMC stranded embroidery thread: 1 skein each Green 469, 472, 502, 734, 890, 907, 3347; Yellow 445, 726, 742, 973

Sewing thread to match the pale yellow hand towel

Small rotating frame or small embroidery hoop

TO MAKE THE DECORATIVE BORDER

1 Mount the short ends of the Hardanger fabric on the rotating sides of the frame, rolling the excess fabric around one of the sides. (If you use an embroidery hoop stretch one end of the strip within it and work this area, removing and repositioning the hoop as necessary.)

2 Use the chart on the left to work the border design, repeating it several times to produce the required length.

3 Use three strands of thread at all times and remember to make all the upper stitches of the Cross Stitches face the same way to produce an even effect. Work each Cross Stitch over two horizontal and two vertical sets of Hardanger fabric threads.

4 Work the design centrally along the strip of fabric until it is long enough to match the width of the hand towel.

5 When the border is complete remove the fabric from the frame and press it gently with a steam iron on the wrong side to encourage the stitchery to stand out on the right side.

890		742
469	907	973
502	472	726
3347	734	445

6 Trim the excess fabric along the sides of the border so that it is approximately 9cm (3½in) wide and that your repeat pattern lies centrally within it.

7 Turn under a narrow hem at the short ends of the border, trimming the excess as necessary. Then pin and baste the border strip across one end of the hand towel.

8 With sewing thread to match the colour of the towel, work machine Satin Stitch along the edges of the border making sure you cover the edges completely and attach the strip to the towel securely.

9 Finally, Slip Stitch the short ends of the border to the sides of the towel to complete this striking hand towel.

SPECIAL TECHNIQUES AND TIPS

As with other forms of decorative stitchery, Cross-Stitch embroidery requires very little in the way of equipment. The techniques and tips explained here are all simple and straightforward processes which will help you to achieve a professional touch when working the projects.

The equipment you will need for working the projects will, I hope, already be found in your sewing basket: a pair of sharp-pointed trimming scissors, larger dressmaking shears, paper-cutting scissors, a good selection of different-sized needles with round points, thimbles, dressmaking pins and needles, a metric or imperial tape measure and ruler, and tacking threads.

If a project does require a special piece of equipment it is noted in the list of materials, so you will not find you get half-way through a project only to discover that you do not possess a cutting knife, for example.

CROSS STITCH

This ancient stitch is worked quickly and simply in two stages, with two diagonal stitches worked over each other to form the cross. Each stitch must be worked in the same way to give a smooth and regular effect, but it does not matter which way the upper stitch of the cross slopes, as long as they all slope in the same direction.

It is a very simple stitch and easily mastered, but do remember that if you are working your embroidery freely, without the use of a frame, there is a risk that you may pull the yarn too tightly when passing the needle through the fabric. This will cause a pinched stitch and uneven tension, which will spoil the overall effect.

The stitches can be worked from right to left, or left to right as you please. For the purpose of the designs in this book where there are often small and irregular areas of one colour, you may work in whichever direction you find easier.

Stitches can be worked as complete stitches (see steps 1 to 3 below), or they may be half-worked in one direction and then completed by working back in the opposite direction (see step 4 below). Remember that your aim is to achieve an even effect of identically formed crosses.

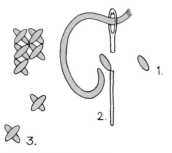

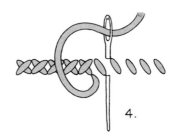

1.= HALF A CROSS STITCH
2.= THE SECOND STITCH OF THE CROSS BEING WORKED
3.= A GROUP OF COMPLETED CROSS STITCHES AND ISOLATED CROSS STITCHES. NOTE: ALL THE UPPER PARTS OF THE CROSS STITCHES LIE IN THE SAME DIRECTION.

4.= A LINE OF CROSS STITCHES WORKED BY STITCHING THE LOWER PARTS OF ALL THE CROSSES, THEN COMPLETING THEM BY RETURNING ALONG THE LINE, WORKING THE UPPER STITCHES.

BACK STITCH

The only other embroidery stitch employed in some of the projects is Back Stitch, and is used to give a thin line which could not be achieved by Cross Stitches, for example where the flowers have fine threadlike roots, as on the Wild Strawberry napkin on page 102.

Remember to work each Back Stitch over the same number of threads as for the Cross Stitches so that you keep the same scale of stitchery.

The stitches can be worked horizontally or vertically on the fabric, as well as diagonally, giving extra freedom of representation.

BACK STITCH IS WORKED OVER THE SAME NUMBER OF THREADS AS THE CROSS STITCHES IN A DESIGN AND IS USED TO GIVE FINE LINES, SUCH AS ROOTS OR OUTLINES OF PETALS WHICH CANNOT BE REPRESENTED BY CROSS STITCHES.

WORKING FROM A CHART

All the designs in the book are charted for you to follow. Every cross on a chart represents a single Cross Stitch on your fabric, and its colour is linked by a key to the colour and type of thread that you should use. Remember that you must work systematically when following a chart, and that it is very important to keep checking that you are reading the chart accurately.

You may find it best to start in the centre for some designs, or at a corner, for example with a border. However, it is always advisable to find and mark the centre of your fabric with Basting Stitches and to have guidelines to help you transfer the design from the chart to the fabric.

FABRICS

Cross-Stitch embroidery can be worked on a great variety of fabrics, although it is easier and usually much more effective to use an evenweave fabric with threads that are easy to see and count. As the name suggests the fabric is evenly constructed with the weft threads passing regularly over and under the warp threads, so that when Cross Stitches are worked the stitches are well-balanced in shape and size.

The fabrics used in the projects are all good quality evenweave embroidery fabrics which are easy to obtain from specialist shops and large department stores. Remember that if you cannot obtain a particular fabric you may still use the design with a different gauge of fabric, just allow more or less yarn, depending on the size of your Cross Stitches.

The following fabrics have been used in this book and each one will produce a totally different effect:

Hardanger is probably one of the most well-known evenweave fabrics. It is finely woven giving 22 stitches per inch or 11 Cross Stitches when worked over two horizontal and two vertical threads. *Pearl Aida* is another well-known fabric woven in a square mesh pattern to give a medium-sized Cross Stitch (11 per inch), see the cushion on page 107. *Fine Aida* is very similar to Pearl Aida, but gives a slightly smaller Cross Stitch (14 per inch), see page 97. *Ainring* is also a type of Aida fabric, but it has a much closer weave, giving a tiny stitch (18 per inch). However, if the Cross Stitches are worked over two sets of horizontal and two vertical sets of threads, you will produce a larger stitch (9 per inch) as in the Daisy Sewing Basket on page 56. *Hertarette* is a large gauge fabric producing a larger stitch (8 Cross Stitches per inch) - see the large pot cover photographed on page 28.

Linda is a finely woven fabric which differs from the other fabrics listed above in that its weft and warp threads are single threads individually woven, unlike the others which are woven in groups or sets. In the projects where Linda is used the Cross Stitches are all worked over two horizontal and two vertical threads to give 14 stitches per inch. The close-up photograph on page 62 shows this fabric extremely clearly.

Mono canvas has been used for the two canvaswork cushions in the Periwinkle and Convolvulus chapters. It is available in several different gauges; for the projects in this book the canvas has 15 holes per inch and the Cross Stitches are worked over two horizontal and two vertical threads so that there are just over 7 stitches per inch.

THREADS AND YARNS

With the growing popularity of needlecrafts and embroidery, there is a similar growth in the availability of all the various threads and yarns that are recommended.

Most of the threads are made of cotton or wool, and the range of colours is extensive.

Always consider the type of thread in relation to the effect you wish to achieve. Some threads can be divided, giving a very fine and delicate effect or a thicker one; others cannot be split, as their fibres are twisted together when they are being spun. Also there is a difference between matt, hairy woollen yarns and the lustrous, shiny effect of cotton yarns. If you are in doubt about the effect you wish to achieve, make a few test stitches on a spare piece of fabric before you begin working on the project.

The following threads are used in the items shown throughout this book:

Stranded thread (sometimes known as embroidery floss) is a slightly lustrous thread of six loosely twisted strands which can be separated and used singly or in any combination.

Coton perlé or *pearl cotton* is a twisted thread with a rich, shiny appearance. It cannot be divided, but is available in three slightly different thicknesses: no. 8, the finest; no. 5, slightly thicker and most commonly available; and no. 3, the thickest.

Soft embroidery cotton is the thickest of the cotton threads, similar to some types of crochet cotton, with a dull, matt finish. It is a very soft thread and cannot be divided.

Tapisserie or tapestry wool is a nondivisible four-ply woollen yarn which is ideal for canvaswork and is available in a vast range of colours.

One of the attractions of Cross Stitch embroidery is that by simply changing the size of your stitch and the thickness of the yarn you can change your design. For example, a very finely worked piece, using two strands of stranded embroidery thread, can become a big, bold design by using a double thickness of tapisserie wool or even rug wool.

EMBROIDERY FRAMES

Using a frame will be very helpful to you, and your embroidery will be more successful and have a professional look when finished if you do. It is not only easier to handle fabric that is held taut within a frame, but you will find your stitches are well-formed. If it is necessary for stitches to be of an even size or spacing, this can be done much more easily by using a frame. Also distortion of the fabric caused by pulling yarn or thread too tightly through the fabric is reduced to an acceptable minimum.

There are a variety of frames available, and the choice depends upon the type of fabric, size of project and personal preference.

If you do not have the exact size of frame available, but have something similar you will probably be able to make use of it. However, if you need to reposition the fabric on the frame while you are working, you must be particularly careful to keep the fabric clean

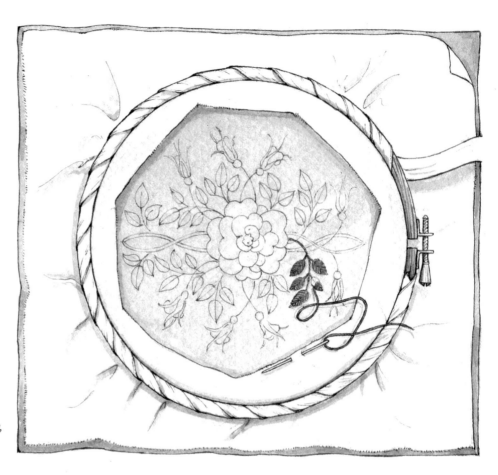

A circular embroidery hoop is ideal for small pieces of stitchery, repeat patterns and borders.

along the edges of the frame as these quickly become marked through handling. A piece of spare fabric pinned over the frame with a cut-out window over the working area will help prevent the fabric from becoming soiled.

Embroidery hoops are used for small pieces of embroidery worked on plainweave fabrics that will not become permanently distorted when pulled taut within the round frame. (Fabrics such as nonwoven felt or needlepoint canvas are unsuitable.)

Wooden hoops are preferable to the less rigid plastic ones, and many different sizes are available. It is advisable to collect several sizes, as they are inexpensive and you can then simply select the most suitable one to use for each project.

Fabric tape wound around the outer ring of the hoop will protect soft fabrics and stitchery from the hard wooden edge. The extra layer of tape will also ensure that you get a taut working area,

as it prevents the fabric from sagging while it is being worked.

Similarly, an extra layer of spare fabric placed on top of the working fabric, mounted in the hoop and then carefully cut away to reveal the area of stitchery, will protect the stitched fabric from the risk of being soiled during handling.

You must be careful when using a circular hoop with evenweave fabric to ensure that the grain of the fabric is straight so that your Cross Stitches do not become distorted in shape.

Rectangular frames are very useful for larger pieces of embroidery and canvas needlepoint. They can be made quickly and simply from lengths of whitewood 2×2cm ($\frac{3}{4} \times \frac{3}{4}$in). The corners can be butted or mitred and held together with wood adhesive glue and nails.

Old, clean picture frames of soft wood can also be useful and inexpensive. Alternatively, use ready-made artists' stretchers.

The fabric is stretched and fastened on this type of frame with staples or drawing pins (thumb tacks). Start at the centre of opposite sides and work towards the corners, carefully pulling and fixing the fabric so that it is evenly taut and secure on the frame.

Specialist frames (slate or rotating frames) are more expensive, but they can be of great use as they are adjustable and you can stretch fabric very evenly on them. They are useful when working a long thin strip of embroidery, such as a border for a towel (see the Periwinkle Guest Towel on pages 86-7 and the Convolulus Hand Towel on page 16) or a tie-back (see the Wood Sorrel Tie-back on pages 74-5).

Using a G-cramp

A carpenter's G-cramp, also known as a C-clamp, can greatly assist you if your embroidery is stretched on a rectangular frame. Without the cramp you have to hold the frame firmly in one hand, leaving only one hand free to stitch with. However, if you fix the frame securely to the edge of a table with the cramp, you will find that both hands are free so that you can stitch much more quickly and feel more comfortable.

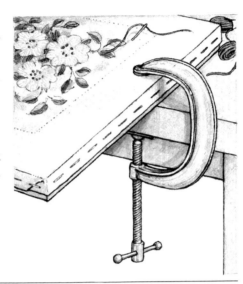

Using a G-cramp: with your frame protruding over the edge of a table and held firmly in place by the G-cramp, you will have both hands free for sewing.

Using a Template

These are simple shapes usually made of thin cardboard or firm paper. They are made by tracing the pattern shape and transferring it to the cardboard. The shape is cut out and then used as a rigid pattern to draw around on fabric.

This method is particularly useful when the same shape is to be repeated several times in a design, for example, in the Daisy Hexagonal Box on page 50.

Enlarging a Design

Some designs can be enlarged to another size for working. This can be done successfully by the following 'grid' method, but accurate measuring is important.

Place the small design within a box and draw a grid of squares over it. Draw a larger box with the same proportions, but of the required size. Draw the same number of bigger squares within this larger box.

Copy the small design, square by square, onto the larger grid, marking where design lines cross grid lines. Join up all these marks. Fill in the now enlarged design with small Cross Stitches. This method allows you to make a small motif into a bold design. By varying the material you work on and the thread used you can also adapt designs for different uses.

A quick way of enlarging a design can be achieved by using a photocopy machine, many of which now have the capacity to change the size of documents and drawings.

Draw a grid of squares over the small design, then draw a diagonal line through the grid, extending it to make a larger box of the same proportions as the small one, but enlarged to the required size.

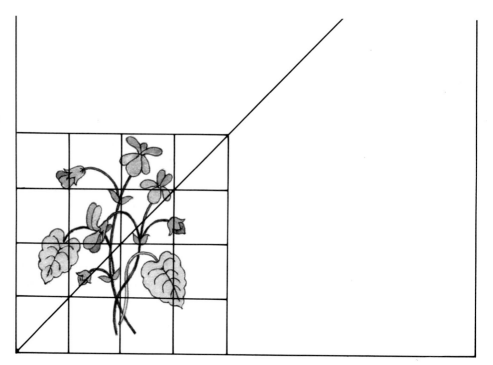

Then draw a grid of the same number of squares in the big box. Copy where the design lines intersect the grid lines and then carefully and accurately join them up to give the enlarged design.

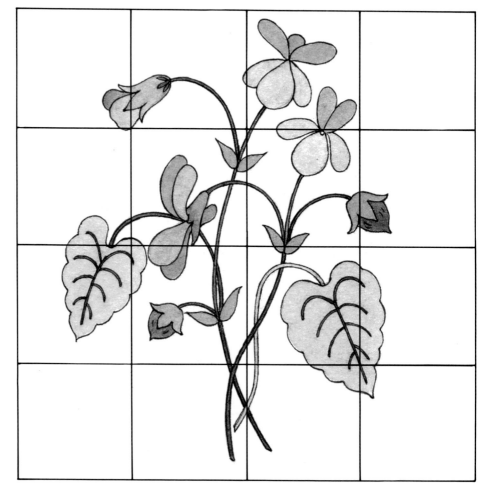

MAKING A GIFT CARD OR GREETINGS CARD

Use thin card that is firm enough to hold fabric within it while standing upright, but also thin enough to be folded easily. Choose the finished size of your gift card, remembering that you must allow a sufficiently wide border of card around the cut-out window to support the fabric.

You will need a piece of thin card large

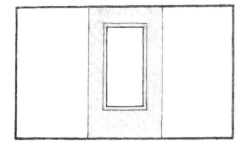

enough to fit the required shape (square or rectangle) within it, plus another of the same dimensions on either side of it.

Lightly score the card dividing it into the three sections and fold along the score lines. Open out the card and accurately measure and mark the cut-out window shape within the centre section. Cut this out using a sharp craft knife. Make sure the window is centrally positioned widthwise, although it may be slightly nearer the top of the card than the bottom edge to give a pleasing effect.

The left-hand section becomes the back of the card and the right-hand section folds over the back of the card front to neaten it and hide the wrong side of the fabric.

MAKING A TWISTED CORD

Twisted cords in the same colour as one of the yarns used in a piece of embroidery will greatly enhance the work, as they will obviously match the colour scheme and yet are easy to make.

Cut three or more lengths of the chosen yarn, 2½ to 3 times the finished length of the cord required. Knot all the lengths together at one end and loop them around a closed door handle (or get a friend to hold them tightly). Knot the other ends together securely and pass a pencil through the loop that has been made. Wind the pencil round and round so that the yarn twists. Continue doing this, keeping the yarn taut until it coils around itself when it is slackened slightly. Then carefully bring the two knotted ends together so that both halves of the yarn twist tightly around

one another. Gently pull and ease the cord until it is evenly twisted. Knot the ends together to prevent them from unravelling.

A thin cord, suitable for edging a cushion or tie-back, can be made by using three lengths of coton perlé no. 5. For a thicker cord, use more lengths of thread, or select a thicker yarn.

To make a two-colour twisted cord use two groups of different coloured thread of the required length and colour. Tie all the threads together close to one end to join them. Then separate the colours so that the knot lies in the centre with one colour on one side of it and the second colour on the other side, and doubling the length of the threads to be twisted. Then knot the loose ends of each colour and make the cord in the usual way.

MAKING A TASSEL

Take a length of thread or yarn 91cm (36in) long. Fold this in half four times to give a bundle of threads (see step 1 overleaf). Take a second length of thread, double it and pass it through a large-eyed needle (see step 2 overleaf).

Hold the double thread around the bundle of threads and pass the needle

through the loop (see step 3 overleaf).

Pull it up tightly, then pass the needle down through the bundle and cut it off at the end of the other threads (see step 4 in the drawings overleaf).

Thread the needle again as before, and take it around the head of the tassel, pass it through the loop, pull it up tightly

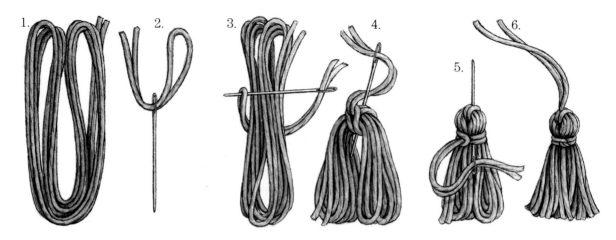

and secure it by pushing the needle up through the head and out at the top of the tassel (see step 5 above).

Do not cut off these threads as they can be used to sew the tassel in place (see step 6 above).

FINISHING TIPS

All the projects in the book include instructions for finishing your embroidery. Generally, you should always remember to handle your stitchery with care, so that the fabric looks fresh and requires the minimum of pressing (if any).

If you do have to press your embroidery, *never* do so on the right side, as it will flatten and spoil the texture and finish of your stitchery. Always press on the wrong side, preferably with a steam iron. Light use of spray starch can also be effective.

If you need to lace your embroidery over a board to make a picture, remember to allow plenty of fabric around each edge of the design area for it to be folded over to the wrong side. Use cardboard that will not bend easily and strong button thread that will not break when pulled tightly.

CARE OF EMBROIDERY

If you have used good quality fabric and threads, your embroidery will last for years and years.

However, there are certain ways of prolonging the life of stitchery. Never place any embroidery in direct sunlight or near strong artificial lights, as both heat and light cause colours to fade and the fibres of fabrics and threads to weaken. Similarly, do not place embroidery near a heat source, as this will also make the stitchery very brittle. Remember, too, that a damp atmosphere can be equally damaging.

Frequent laundering should be avoided if at all possible and always use a mild cleaning agent. Gently reshape the article while damp and do not allow it to dry out completely before pressing it on the wrong side with a steam iron.

If you need to clean a cushion or some other article that may not be totally colourfast, then dry cleaning is essential.

Care for your embroidery as though it is an heirloom in the making. Enjoy it, respect it, but equally do not hide it away. Folding it and sealing it in a plastic bag will cause permanent creases which will in time weaken and break. Also, the lack of air will prevent the fibres from breathing.

If you must store your work for a long period of time, it is better if it can be stored flat or rolled smoothly (right side out), in layers of protective, acid-free tissue paper. Then it should be placed in a clean fabric cover such as a pillowcase, and finally placed somewhere dark, dry and, of course, moth-free.

134

STOCKISTS AND SUPPLIERS

Dunlicraft Ltd, Pullman Road,
Wigston, Leicester LE8 2DY
*(DMC threads and yarns, Zweigart
evenweave fabrics, canvas,
information and lists of stockists)*

John Lewis, 278–306 Oxford Street,
London W1A 1EX
(Cotton fabrics, towelling, baskets)

Liberty, 210–220 Regent Street,
London W1R 6AH
(Plain and patterned cotton fabrics)

Laura Ashley Ltd, P.O. Box 19,
Newtown, Powys, Wales SY16 4BR
(Plain and patterned cotton fabrics)

C. M. Offray & Son Ltd,
Fir Tree Place, Church Road,
Ashford, Middlesex TW15 2PH
(Ribbons)

DMC Corporation,
107 Trumbull Street, Elizabeth,
New Jersey 07206
(DMC threads and yarns)

Joan Toggitt Ltd,
35 Fairfield Place, West Caldwell,
New Jersey 07006
(Zweigart fabrics)

ACKNOWLEDGEMENTS

There are too many people who have helped in the creation of this book to mention everyone by name, but I would like to thank the following in particular.

Jacky Boase once more managed to find ideal locations for every photograph, whether it was a hedgerow or a field of daisies, every one of which was sympathetic to my embroidery. Also many thanks to her friends who so willingly allowed the photographs to be taken in their gardens: Sue Day, Sue Greenwood, David Laffeatty, Jane Sheppard, Carmel Sturridge and Mary Taylor.

Thanks to Julie Fisher for her superb photography, to Clare Clements for her delightful book design, and to Colin Salmon for painstakingly working the charts.

I would like to thank everyone at Dunlicraft Ltd for their generous support and limitless supply of fabrics and threads which I used throughout the book.

Thanks to Jane Judd, my agent; to Sarah Wallace and Valerie Buckingham at Century for all their encouragement and sympathetic support.

Finally, I would like to thank Dan, and, of course, our daughter Sarah Jane, for being so 'well behaved' during the creation of the book; and for waiting so patiently for me to finish writing the book before being born.

INDEX

Page numbers in *italic* denote illustrations.

137